What Really Matters in Vocabulary

Research-Based Practices across the Curriculum

Patricia M. Cunningham

Wake Forest University

PEARSON

Boston • New York • San Francisco
Mexico City • Montreal • Toronto • London • Madrid • Munich • Paris
Hong Kong • Singapore • Tokyo • Cape Town • Sydney

Executive Editor: Aurora Martínez Ramos
Series Editorial Assistant: Kara Kikel
Marketing Manager: Danae April
Production Editor: Annette Joseph
Editorial Production Service: Lynda Griffiths
Composition Buyer: Linda Cox
Manufacturing Buyer: Linda Morris
Electronic Composition: Denise Hoffman
Interior Design: Denise Hoffman
Cover Designer: Kristina Mose-Libon

For Professional Development resources, visit www.allynbaconmerrill.com.

Between the time website information is gathered and then published, it is not unusual for some sites to have closed. Also, the transcription of URLs can result in typographical errors. The publisher would appreciate notification where these errors occur so that they may be corrected in subsequent editions.

ISBN-10: 0-205-57041-0
ISBN-13: 978-0-205-57041-6

Printed in the United States of America

10 9 8 7 6 5 4 3 2 1   RRD-VA 12 11 10 09 08

Allyn & Bacon
is an imprint of

www.pearsonhighered.com

Contents

Preface

Vocabulary is a topic about which there is much talk and little action. Everyone knows that developing students' vocabularies is a critical goal in all subject areas, but the task seems so enormous that most of us don't know where to begin. Today, as in years past, the most common vocabulary activity in classrooms consists of having students look up words, copy definitions, put words in sentences, and learn the words for the vocabulary test. When asked, most of us acknowledge that these traditional vocabulary activities probably don't accomplish much. But what is the alternative? How do we increase the number of words students know meanings for as well as the depth of meanings for those words as a day-in, day-out, across-the-school-day priority?

I wrote this book to address the lack of vocabulary instruction in our elementary schools. I am concerned about all the students we teach, but I am most concerned about the ever-increasing number of students we teach who are not native English speakers and about children who live in economic poverty. The gap between the "haves" and "have-nots" in the United States affects all areas of schooling, but this gap is most apparent when looking at the differences in vocabulary—words students have meanings for and the depth of meanings they have for those words. In this book, I have gathered the most effective and "do-able" vocabulary instructional activities and provided examples and suggestions of how teachers can include these activities as they carry out instruction across the curriculum. I believe that if these activities are implemented all day, every day, we can make progress in closing the wide vocabulary gap that exists in the Unites States today.

Thank you to the following reviewers for their comments and suggestions: Amanda Arens, Arens Consulting; Tensil Clayton, Curriculum Supervisor, Grades 4–12, Martin County, North Carolina; Eve Hayes; Sharon Moore, Osborn School District; and Debi Porter.

The **What Really Matters** *Series*

The past decade or so has seen a dramatic increase in the interest in what the research says about reading instruction. Much of this interest was stimulated by several recent federal education programs: the Reading Excellence Act of 1998, the No Child Left Behind Act of 2001, and the Individuals with Disabilities Education Act of 2004. The commonality shared by these federal laws is that each law restricts the use of federal funds to instructional services and support that have been found to be effective through "scientific research."

In this new series we bring you the best research-based instructional advice available. In addition, we have cut through the research jargon and at least some of the messiness and provide plain-language guides for teaching students to read. Our focus is helping you use the research as you plan and deliver instruction to your students. Our goal is that your lessons be as effective as we know how, given the research that has been published.

Our aim is that all children become active and engaged readers and that all develop the proficiencies needed to be strong independent readers. For us, strong independent readers are active and comprehending readers. Each of the short books in this series features what we know about one aspect of teaching and learning to read independently with understanding. Each of these pieces is important to this goal but none is more important than the ultimate goal: active, strong, independent readers who read with understanding.

So, enjoy these books and teach your students all to read.

chapter 1
Why Vocabulary Matters

*M*eaning *vocabulary* is an intensely personal topic for me. The second year of my career found me teaching first grade in a large rural school 20 miles north of Tallahassee, Florida. All the children were bused to school from the surrounding plantations. Few if any parents ever came to school, having no way to get there.

On the first day of school, I looked out at 32 children left at my door by older brothers, sisters, and cousins. (Fortunately, these older children also gathered the first-graders from my room at the end of the day since neither I nor my students had any idea what bus they should ride!) At the end of the first day, I was supposed to send a "roll" of my students to the office. I knew I had 32 students but I had only 29 names. Who were those other 3 children who had spent their first day of school in my classroom? (Florida had no public kindergarten at that time.) On the following morning, I put a name tag on all children as they came in the door, spelling the names they told me as best I could. One child would not talk to me and no one in the class seemed to know who he was. At the end of that day I sent a roll with 31 names and one question mark. Needless to say, I was called to the office and ordered to supply the name of that student! The next morning, I stood at my door as the big kids dropped off the little ones. When I spotted the nameless child, I quickly nabbed the older brother and succeeded at getting a name to write on the name tag. Three days into the school year, I triumphantly sent a roll with names attached to my 32 students—although I had no confidence I had all those names spelled correctly!

Our school followed a very traditional curriculum. We had a math series with a workbook and a basal reading series with a six-week "readiness" program. I taught my children to count and recognize numbers. We learned letter names and sounds and auditory discrimination (very similar to what is now called phonemic awareness). The children were attentive and eager, and although no child knew these concepts before coming to school, some of them learned them remarkably fast. My biggest challenge and frustration was with their extremely limited vocabularies. This became obvious to me immediately because the readiness workbooks had page after page of pictures to which the children were supposed to attach beginning sounds. On a page with lots of **m** pictures, all the children could name the **man** and the **milk**. Some could name the **mop**, **moon**, **monkey**, and **motorcycle**. Everyone called the **mouse** a "rat." No one was able to name the **map**, **moose**, **mule**, or **mirror**. Math provided another daily example of my students' meager vocabulary stores. Most children understood the concept of counting and numbers such as 1, 2, and 3. Almost no one made any connections to ordinal numbers **first**, **second**, **third**, and so on. Position words were very frustrating for my first-graders. Most knew **over** and **under** but **above**, **below**, **behind**, **left**, and **right** were simply not part of their vocabularies.

When I became aware of how meager the vocabularies of almost all my students were, I started making lists of words I needed to teach. Knowing that the best way to teach words was with real objects, I raided my apartment and the apartments of my friends and carted in objects whenever I could. As I began to gather the objects, I realized that one example object is almost never enough. My mop at home was the squeeze type; the mop pictured in the readiness book was a "stringy" mop. The mirror I took off my wall at home bore little resemblance to the hand-held mirror pictured. Having a concept for "mop" and "mirror" was clearly much broader than any one example. Many things could not be represented by objects, so I found my picture file, assiduously collected during all my undergraduate education courses. This was of some help, but I had not a single picture of a motorcycle, mule, or moose! I haunted yard sales, grabbing old magazines and encyclopedias, and expanded my picture file. (Never did I imagine at that time being able to download and print images from the Web.)

Each time I tried to build concepts for words on my list, I discovered more words my students didn't know. **Moose** live in **herds** and have **antlers**. A **mule** is part **donkey** and has **hooves**. What you see in the **mirror** is your **reflection**. Sometimes the **moon** is **full** and sometimes it is a **half** or **quarter** moon. (I am sure I did not convince some of my children that there actually is *not* a man in the moon!)

Another complication in my attempt to build meaning vocabularies became evident when a child announced that Jackson didn't come to school today because he got "bus left." "That's right," confirmed another child. Since I had diligently been working on the concepts of "left" and "right"—left hand, right hand; left side, right side—I recognized some other entirely different meanings for these words. Once I became aware of how many common words had two or more very different meanings, these multimeaning words were everywhere! The lines on their handwriting paper had little to do with the lines we formed to go to the playground. Being second in line had little to do with the 60 seconds in a minute. The letters we were trying so hard to learn names and sounds for were not like the letters received from grandmothers and aunts. There was also confusion with words that are spelled differently but sound exactly the same to children who are just learning the word meanings.

"Were you the **one** who **won** the race?"

"The coach **blew** the **blue** whistle."

"Yesterday we **read** the **red** book."

Every day my list of vocabulary I needed to teach grew longer and longer as new words, words connected to previous words, multiple meanings, and homophones were added. Finally, the list got so long that I gave it up! I realized that I would never be able to directly teach all the words my students needed. But I worried. How were they ever going to learn them?

I gave up writing down the words on the list but I did not give up the constant day-in and day-out battle to increase the size of the children's meaning vocabularies. To build their vocabularies, I relied on three activities: reading to the children, using a wide variety of visuals, and studying real objects.

I read to the children every day from picture books and used the pictures in the books as opportunities for vocabulary development. I discovered that pictures not only worked for nouns but could also help me build other concepts. When a character in a book was angry, we talked about (and mimicked) the expression on that character's face. We also came up with other words for angry such as **mad** and **furious**. A few weeks later, when Rumpelstiltskin flew into a rage when the queen guessed his name, we concluded that when you "fly into a rage," you are really angry, mad, and furious. Pictures can also be used to teach describing words. For example, I would ask the students if they could tell by looking at a picture if the weather was cloudy, sunny, or rainy. Reading a picture book about animals, we talked about how the animals moved, and later, on the playground, we galloped, hopped, and scampered.

I continued to scavenge everywhere for pictures to add to my picture file and I also found some filmstrips that connected to some of our science and social studies topics. On special occasions, I took some Polaroid photographs of the children doing various activities and labeled and posted these. (I never imagined at that time what could be done with a digital camera!) My best teaching friend, Elaine, taught second grade across the hall and she occasionally got movies from the Tallahassee public library. We crowded both our classes into her classroom, popped popcorn, and had a movie party. We stopped the movie regularly and asked the question the children were now familiar with: "Do you know what we call this?" This was a very special treat for the students, most of whom did not have televisions and almost none of whom had ever gone to a movie.

The third daily staple of our vocabulary-building diet was real objects. The children and I named every single thing in the room, including the parts of things: "Doors have knobs and hinges. What else has knobs? Hinges?" "The part around the door is the frame. What other kinds of frames do you see in the room?" Each day the children went home with an assignment to see what things we named in our room they could find in their homes. To their delight, all the children discovered that their houses had doors, knobs, hinges, and frames! When we had about exhausted naming the things in our classroom, we branched out to the cafeteria, the auditorium, the office (on a day when the principal, who was less than sympathetic, was at a staff meeting downtown). Next, we took "naming walks" outside the school. We named trees and parts of trees—branches, leaves, roots, bark, and so on. One of the children realized that dogs bark too and everyone started to try to think of other meanings.

> "The **leaves** on the trees are not like when you **leave** somewhere."
>
> "There are **rocks** here and you can **rock** in a **rocking** chair."
>
> "And **rock** music and you can **rock** around the clock!"

Unfortunately, there were many things not available in our school environment and for which pictures were not particularly helpful. Our basal reading series featured two suburban children, Janet and Mark, and their dog, Socks. The stories were quite appealing but often had the children going places that my students could not even imagine. In one story the children in the reader went to a department store and rode the escalator. Imagine trying to explain escalator to children whose concept of stairs is the three steps going up to their porch! In another story, the textbook characters went to the park, sailed boats in a pond, and rode on the seesaw. Also, Janet and Mark went with their grandparents to a restaurant and ordered food from the menu, which is brought to them by the waitress. I doubt that any of my students had been to a park or a restaurant. Building concepts and vocabulary for the selections in our basal reader was a daily source of frustration for me.

As the year was coming to a close, Elaine and I connived to take our children on a fieldtrip to Tallahassee, which was 25 minutes away and which almost none of the children had ever been to. It was not easy but we corralled a school bus to take us and the cafeteria packed lunches for us all. Somehow, we got permission slips signed and returned, and on a hot Thursday in May, we boarded the bus and headed to the big city! We began in a department store and spent quite a long time riding up and down the escalator. We didn't eat in a restaurant but we did walk through and observe the menus and waitresses. We had lunch in the park where we sailed boats in the pond and rode on a seesaw. The next day, we reread the stories in which Janet and Mark rode the escalator in the department store, lunched in a restaurant, and

played in the park. "Better late than never," I thought as the children finally comprehended and connected to what they were reading in the book.

I hope the children learned as much from me that year as I learned from them. Like most teachers, I did my best but I knew my best was not good enough. From that early teaching experience, I learned firsthand how much meaning vocabulary matters and how complex it was to teach children meanings for words.

In many ways, things are better today in schools for children who used to be called "underprivileged" and "disadvantaged." Every state now has public kindergarten and pre-K available for many needy children. The Web and other technologies make "bringing words to life" a richer and more obtainable goal. As I write this, teachers still have many children coming to school with impoverished vocabularies. Many of these children come from poor families and many do not come with much English. Using every available resource to build rich meaning vocabularies for these children is key to ensuring their success in school and in life. There is no way to overstate the importance of meaning vocabulary to comprehension. The size of a person's vocabulary is one of the best predictors of how well he or she will comprehend while listening or reading. Simply stated, having a bigger vocabulary makes you a better reader.

❊ How Many Words?

How many words do you know?

5,000?
10,000?
20,000?
50,000?
100,000?

If you found it difficult to estimate the size of your vocabulary, you should be comforted to know that this seemingly "simple" question of how many words you know is a difficult one to answer. The first issue is, of course, what is meant by "know"? Is it enough to know that **anthropoids** are some kind of apes or do you have to have the specific information that anthropoids are apes without tails, such as chimpanzees, gorillas, orangutans, and gibbons?

The next question is how many meanings of the word do you have to know? If you know the sports meaning of **coach**, do you also have to know the motorbus and "coach class" meanings to count this word in your meaning vocabulary? The other complication in counting words you have meanings for is how you count the various forms of a word. If **work, works, worked, working, worker, workout, workbook, unworkable,** and **workroom** count as separate words, your vocabulary is much larger than if these words count as one word, all related to the root word **work**.

All these variables—word depth, multimeaning words, and how to count words with the same root—result in wide differences in the estimate of vocabulary size. In spite of the difficulties of estimating vocabulary size, it is important for teachers to have an idea of what the meaning vocabulary development goal is. Biemiller (2004) estimates that entering kindergartners have meanings for an average of 3,500 root words. They add approximately 1,000 root word meanings each school year. The average high school graduate knows about 15,000 root words.

Other vocabulary experts (Graves, 2006; Stahl & Nagy, 2006) argue that Biemiller's estimate is way too low. They believe that words with multiple meanings should be counted as separate words and that many children do not recognize words with common roots. Furthermore, they believe that proper nouns—such as Canada, Abraham Lincoln, and London—should be included in the total word count. When counted in this way, these experts argue that the average child learns 2,000 to 3,000 word meanings each school year and that the average high school graduate has meanings for 40,000 to 50,000 words. Regardless of which estimates you believe, the number of new words children need to add to their vocabularies each year is staggering.

Children differ greatly, however, in the size of their meaning vocabularies at school entrance and as they continue through the grades. These differences in vocabulary size are not random but rather are closely related to socioeconomic status. In 1995, Hart and Risley found that children of professional parents were exposed to 50 percent more words than children from working-class homes. When compared to children in families receiving Aid to Families with Dependent Children, children of professional parents were exposed to twice as many words. Hart and Risley concluded that children from the most affluent homes had vocabularies five times as large as children from the lowest-income homes and that the most important difference in families was the amount of talking that went on. The gap in meaning vocabulary begins early and often continues to widen as children move through school.

Another group of students who come to school with much smaller than average meaning vocabularies are children whose first language is not English. Cummins (1994) states that although children whose first language is not English can often develop fluency in conversational English in a year or two, it takes five or more years for children to bridge the gap and become fluent in the academic English required to succeed in all areas of the school curriculum.

Another reason that the size of a child's meaning vocabulary is crucial to school success is that vocabulary knowledge is cumulative. The more words you know at any point in time, the more words you are able to add to your vocabulary. Shefelbine (1990) investigated children's ability to infer meanings of words from context. Many children with limited vocabularies could not use context clues to figure out meanings for new words because they lacked meanings for many of the words that comprised the context! Children who enter school with small vocabularies tend to add fewer words each year than children who enter with larger vocabularies.

How Do They Learn All Those Words?

To help you understand how we add words to our meaning vocabulary stores, consider the analogy that learning word meanings is a lot like getting to know people. As with words, you know some people extremely well, you are well acquainted with others, you have only vague ideas of still others, and so on. Knowledge of people depends on the experiences you have with them. You know some people, such as family members and close friends, extremely well because you have spent most of your life in their company. You have participated with them regularly in situations that have been intense and emotional as well as routine. At the other extreme, think of people that you have only heard about, as well as historical figures such as Charles Darwin and Catherine the Great and current public figures such as politicians and entertainers. You have heard of them and seen pictures and videos of them, but these people are known only through the secondhand reports of others. Your knowledge of people that you know indirectly through secondhand information is limited in comparison to those you know directly through firsthand experience. Learning words—like coming to know people—varies according to how much time you spend with them and the types of experiences you share.

Now think of how you make new friends. Social gatherings such as parties and meetings are excellent opportunities for getting to know others. When you move through a gathering on your own, you strike up conversations and get to know new people in part as a function of your motivation and your social skills. However, having a host, hostess, or friend introduce you to people tends to expedite the process. Then, once you have made new contacts, you might get to know those individuals better as you meet again in other settings. And don't forget the power of social networking: The more people you know, the more opportunities you have for helping each other out and meeting even more people.

Are you a "people person"? Do you know someone who you would describe as a "people person"? A people person is someone who genuinely likes people and finds them fascinating. A people person is always seeking out new individuals and making new friends. Of course, a people person knows a lot more people than those of us who are a little shyer and more reserved.

Levels of knowledge about people and the dynamics of getting to know them are comparable in many ways to learning words. When given the opportunity, students learn new words on their own, depending on their motivation and literacy skills. Students also benefit from direct introductions and intensive interactions with some new words. As students learn new words, their opportunities for learning additional words increase exponentially. Some students are "word people." They enjoy encountering a new word and are eager to add interesting words to their vocabularies. When they meet a new word, they think about how it is different from other words they know and are eager to try out this new word in discussions with their friends. This fascination with new words is often called "word consciousness" or "word wonder." Students who have so-called word wonder get to know a lot more words— just as a people person knows a lot more people.

How Should We Teach Vocabulary?

Literacy experts all agree on the need for vocabulary building for all students in all grades. There has been a lot of disagreement, however, about the best way to provide students with the valuable vocabulary tools they need. Some experts argue that since students need to learn so many new words each year, and since we cannot possibly teach 1,000 to 3,000 new words well, we would be better off spending our time teaching students how to learn words independently from their reading and providing time and encouragement for large amounts of independent reading. Other experts argue that when words are thoroughly taught, they do increase comprehension of text containing those words, and therefore direct teaching of vocabulary is important even though the number of words we can reasonably teach well is limited.

Everyone agrees that developing in all students a sense of word wonder will result in increased vocabulary learning. Because independent learning of vocabulary, direct teaching of selected words, and developing word wonder all contribute to vocabulary growth, students who are lucky enough to experience quality instruction in all three approaches are apt to develop the largest vocabularies. Thus, as in so many other areas of the elementary curriculum, we must "roll up our sleeves" and "do it all." To be effective, vocabulary development has to be an "all day, every day" pervasive part of the curriculum. Rather than having a separate vocabulary period, we must weave rich vocabulary instruction in all that we do. This book presents a comprehensive vocabulary framework for the elementary classroom. This framework is based on the following principles:

- Students develop meanings for words through multiple and varied encounters with those words.

- Vocabulary is learned best when it is based on real, concrete experiences.

- Pictures and other visuals help solidify word meanings.

- To truly own a word, children must use that word in speaking and writing.

- A set of essential words, including content vocabulary, should be directly taught.

- Because most new words are learned through reading, teacher read-aloud and independent reading time should be scheduled into every elementary student's day.

- Students should be taught strategies for learning new words independently from reading, including instruction in word parts, context, and effective use of the dictionary.

- Instruction should include activities that develop word wonder and exclude ineffective, de-motivating activities such as copying and memorizing definitions and writing vocabulary words in sentences.

✦ What Happens Where and When?

The problem with trying to implement a comprehensive vocabulary framework in a classroom is what to do when and how to fit it in. The remaining chapters of this book will describe how the goals of "all-day, every day" vocabulary instruction can be accomplished across the school day.

Chapter 2 will describe classroom-tested strategies that will motivate all students to engage in more independent reading and ways to maximize the amount of vocabulary students learn during the daily teacher read-aloud time. In order to learn word meanings independently, students must be able to use the pictures, context, and word part cues simultaneously. Modeling the use of picture and context clues is part of the teacher read-aloud procedures described in Chapter 2. The chapter also includes specific strategies for helping students use word part, picture, and context clues as they do their independent reading.

Chapter 3 focuses on teaching all students how to use word parts—prefixes, suffixes, and roots—to "sniff out" the meanings of new words. Instruction in word structure is not generally a very motivating or engaging experience. To make this vocabulary instruction more lively, some of the activities will focus on sports themes and sports words. Students will participate in hunting and gathering words with useful word parts.

Introducing vocabulary before reading a selection is an everyday occurrence in most elementary classrooms. There are two reasons this vocabulary introduction is not apt to increase the number of vocabulary words most students know. First, in order for words to be added to vocabulary, students need to have several different encounters with the words across several days or weeks. Because the words being introduced for a selection are not likely to occur again in other selections, students do not have enough opportunities to encounter the words and make the words their own. The second reason much vocabulary instruction in reading lessons is not effective is because it is seen by the students (and teachers) as boring! Vocabulary introduction, putting words in sentences, and copying definitions is probably the biggest deterrent to students' developing word wonder! Chapter 4 describes engaging ways to maximize the effectiveness of vocabulary instruction during reading lessons. Students will learn to use pictures to anticipate words they might encounter and to use pictures, context, and word parts to figure out meanings for new words.

Vocabulary can be built into the everyday elementary curriculum. Each day elementary children learn math, science, and social studies and participate in

the arts and physical education. These academic content areas each have their own vocabularies, and the key words are used throughout the unit or sometimes across the entire year. Many experts suggest that most direct vocabulary instruction should take place in these academic content areas. Robert Marzano (2004), an advocate for the direct teaching of important vocabulary terms in all content areas, has developed an extensive list of 7,923 critical terms for all subjects K–12. Chapters 5, 6, 7, and 8 of this book will provide grade-specific lists of core vocabulary in math, science, social studies, the arts, and physical education, along with specific vocabulary strategies for teaching the different words in the different content areas. Strategies for making sure students have multiple and varied encounters with the words, for using real concrete experiences and visuals to build meanings for words, and for getting children to use the words in discussions, drawing, and writing will be described.

The final chapter of this book provides games, activities, and selected children's books that teachers can use to help students develop their word consciousness and become "word people" who can't wait to encounter and befriend the next new word!

The number of children in the classroom whose first language is not English continues to grow every year. Recent estimates suggest that approximately 19 percent of all students are English language learners. In many school districts, that number is much higher. Of all English language learners, approximately 79 percent are Spanish speaking. Almost every teacher now has children who are learning English as they are mastering all the other goals of the elementary school curriculum. Obviously, these children come with smaller English vocabularies and their limited vocabularies limit their learning in all subject areas. Throughout this book, suggestions are included for adaptations teachers can make to boost the meaning vocabularies of English language learners.

Research Support for a Comprehensive Vocabulary Instructional Program

Most research studies of vocabulary instruction have been short-term interventions focused on one particular aspect of vocabulary. Often these studies were conducted in a laboratory rather than a classroom setting. A study published in the October 2007 issue of *The Reading Teacher* (Bauman, Ware, & Carr Edwards) was conducted in a fifth-grade classroom across the entire school year and measured the effect of a comprehensive vocabulary development program. The study was carried out in a diverse low-income school in which 65 percent of the students qualified for free/reduced price lunch. The multifaceted vocabulary program was modeled on that outlined by Graves (2006) and included the four components he identified as effective:

1. Providing rich and varied language experiences
2. Teaching individual words
3. Teaching word learning (morphology, context, dictionary) strategies
4. Fostering word consciousness

The article includes a rich description of the classroom instruction included to assure students were engaged in vocabulary learning that includes all four components. To provide rich and varied language experiences, the teacher read to the students daily and focused on the vivid vocabulary found in the rich literature. During their daily independent reading time, students recorded "new, interesting and unusual" words they found in their reading. Weekly dialogue journals provided the teacher an opportunity to support and encourage students' discovery of new words in their reading. The use of "strong words" was also modeled and encouraged as students engaged in daily writing workshops.

To teach individual words, the teacher relied heavily on a vocabulary wall to which students and teacher added interesting words. Students also did self-assessments of how well they knew key words chosen by the teacher before reading selections and then worked with these words using a variety of graphic organizers and other activities that required students to categorize words and determine shades of meaning. The teaching of individual words occurred as part of the regular reading instruction and instruction in all curriculum areas.

Word learning strategy instruction included lessons on common prefixes, suffixes, and roots, and students were encouraged to add example words to a class chart. Instruction on various types of context clues and how to use a dictionary to clarify the meaning of a word was also included throughout the year.

Word consciousness was fostered as students engaged in a variety of word-play activities and sought out instances of metaphorical and figurative language. For one activity designed to enhance word consciousness, students interviewed parents and grandparents to discover what kind of slang was used by previous generations and created a class chart of old slang, including "toodle-loo" for good-bye and "been there, done that" for already been through that.

To determine the effectiveness of this year-long comprehensive vocabulary program, students' vocabularies were measured at the beginning and end of the year using both receptive and expressive vocabulary instruments. In addition, students completed assessments designed to measure their interest in vocabulary and parents indicated how often their students talked about learning new vocabulary.

At the end of the year, students demonstrated vocabulary growth on both quantitative and qualitative measures. Their expressive (speaking) vocabularies grew more than expected in one year's time. Their receptive (listening) vocabularies also grew and this growth was greater for students who started the year with smaller receptive vocabularies. A comparison of writing samples from the beginning and end of the year indicated that students used 36 percent more words and 42 percent more low-frequency words in their end-of-the-year writing sample. Qualitative results indicated that students' aptitude toward learning new words increased, as did their ability to use word learning strategies and their willingness to engage in word play.

I include this description of this year-long classroom study of multi-faceted vocabulary instruction in the hopes that it will inspire you as it has me. It is logical to believe that a comprehensive program of vocabulary development across the curriculum will improve vocabulary, and this study provides evidence of its effectiveness. It is important to keep in mind that the fifth-graders in this classroom were mostly from low-income homes—the very students most affected by the vocabulary gap. There is no simple or quick fix for increasing the size and depth of students' vocabularies. As you read and think about how to implement a comprehensive across-the-curriculum vocabulary program in your classroom, have confidence that your efforts will reap rich rewards!

chapter 2

Maximizing Vocabulary Growth from Reading

The number of words in your meaning vocabulary store is directly related to how much you read. Children who read the most have the biggest vocabularies. Children who read only when they are assigned something to read have smaller vocabularies.

Children who like to read and are good readers read much more than children who don't like to read and who struggle with reading. This connection between how well you read, how much you read, and vocabulary size is well known but its implications for daily classroom life are often ignored. Many teachers just accept the fact that their struggling readers don't like to read and avoid reading whenever possible. Because of the clear relationship between meaning vocabulary size and volume of reading, accepting the idea that "some kids just don't like to read" means those kids will never become good readers!

There is a vicious cycle here that begins when children come to school with few print experiences and small meaning vocabularies. These children struggle with learning to read. Because reading is hard for them, they avoid reading. But, since reading is one of the major ways new words are learned, the meaning vocabulary gap between children who like to read and read well and children who struggle with reading grows wider every day. Children who come to school with rich meaning vocabularies read more and add more words to their vocabularies. Children who come to school with impoverished meaning vocabularies read less and add fewer words. If there is any hope of truly "closing the gap" in literacy, we must all commit ourselves to making reading something all our students enjoy and choose! Children cannot all read at the same level but they can all learn to find pleasure in reading.

What can you do to create a whole class of children who like to read? The answer to that question is simple and straightforward. You read to children every day from a wide variety of types of books, magazines, and newspapers. You provide time every day for children to read whatever they choose to read. You provide access to the widest possible range of reading materials. You arrange for regular opportunities for children to share what they are reading with you and with their friends.

✾ Assess and Document Your Students' Independent Reading

If having all your students reading more and with greater enthusiasm is one of your most important goals, you are more likely to achieve that goal if you know where the children are early in the year and how they are progressing toward that goal. Many teachers do a "status" assessment early in the year to determine how children feel about themselves as readers. They file these away and then have the children respond to the same questions halfway through the year and at the end of the year. After the children assess themselves halfway through the year, give them the report they completed early in the year and have them compare how they are "growing up" as readers. File both the early report and the midyear report. At the end of the year, have children self-report their reading habits one last time. After completing the final report, give them the first and second reports and have them write a paragraph summarizing their change and growth as readers. Many children are amazed (and proud!) to see how much more they like to read. The Me and Reading form is one example of the type of questions you might use to help you and your students assess the status of their growth as readers.

Me and Reading

My name is _____.

Here is how I feel about reading as of _____ (today's date).

The best book I ever read is _____.

I like it because _____.

The best book I read in the last 4 months is _____.

I like it because _____.

My favorite author is _____.

My favorite kind of book is _____.

When I am home, I read: (Circle one)

Almost never   Sometimes   Almost every day   Every day

This is how I feel about reading right now: (Circle one)

I love reading.   I like reading OK.   I don't like reading.   I hate reading.

✣ Make Teacher Read-Aloud an Everyday Event

Teacher read-aloud has been shown to be one of the major motivators for children's desire to read. In 1975, Sterl Artley asked successful college students what they remembered their teachers doing that motivated them to read. The majority of students responded that teachers reading aloud to the class was what got them interested in reading. More recently, elementary students were asked what motivated them to read particular books. The most frequent response was "My teacher read it to the class" (Palmer, Codling, & Gambrell, 1994). Ivey and Broaddus (2001) surveyed 1,765 sixth-graders to determine what motivates them to read. The responses of this large group of diverse preteens indicated that their major motivation for reading came from having time for independent reading of books of their own choosing and teachers reading aloud to them.

Reading aloud to children is a simple and research-proven way to motivate children of all ages to become readers. When thinking about our struggling readers, however, we need to also consider what the teacher is reading aloud. Did you know that most of the fiction sold in bookstores is sold to women and most of the informational books are sold to men? Now, this doesn't mean that women never read informational texts or that men never read fiction, it just means that there does seem to be a preference among males for information.

Reading aloud stimulates motivation and what we read aloud may really matter to struggling readers. In *True Stories from Four Blocks Classrooms,* Deb Smith (2001) describes her daily teacher read-aloud session. Each day Deb reads one chapter from a fiction book, a part of an informational book, and an "everyone" book. She chooses the "everyone" book by looking for a short, simple book that "everyone in my class will enjoy and can read." (She *never* calls these books easy books!) By reading from these three types of books daily, Deb demonstrates to her students that all kinds of books are cherished and acceptable in her classroom. Deb follows her teacher read-aloud with independent reading time. The informational books and the "everyone" books are popular choices—especially with her boys who struggle with reading.

Reading aloud to students is more common in primary grades than in upper grades even though it might be more important for teachers of older

children to read aloud. Most children develop the reading habit between the ages of 8 and 11. Reading aloud to older children provides the motivation for them to read at the critical point when they have the literacy skills to take advantage of that motivation. Teachers of older children can show the children the whole range of things that adults read by making an extra effort to bring real-world reading materials such as newspapers and magazines into the classroom and to read tidbits from these with an "I was reading this last night and I just couldn't wait to get here and share it with you" attitude. Intermediate teachers need to make a special effort to read books from all the different sections of the bookstore. Most of us who are readers established our reading preferences in those preteen years. If we read *Cam Jensen* mysteries then, we probably still enjoy reading mysteries today. If we read *Star Wars* and *Star Trek* books then, we probably still enjoy science fiction today. If we packed biographies of famous people and informational books about sports to take to camp, the books we pack in our vacation travel bag today are probably still more information than fiction.

One way you can motivate more of your students to become readers is to read some books in a series and some books by authors who have written lots of other books. Remember that your students often want to read the book you read aloud. Read aloud one of the David Adler's *Cam Jensen* mysteries and then show your students several more Cam Jensen mysteries that you wish you had time to read aloud to them. Read aloud one of Gail Gibbons's informational books on animals—perhaps *Sharks* or *Whales* or *Dogs*—and then show the children the other 40 you wish you had time to read to them. Your students who like mysteries may have "choice anxiety" trying to decide which *Cam Jensen* mystery they want to read first, and your animal-lover informational readers will not know where to begin with all of Gail Gibbons's wonderful animal books. Unlike most anxiety, this kind of choice anxiety is a good thing!

Maximize Vocabulary Growth through Teacher Read-Aloud

Teacher read-aloud is one of the major opportunities for children to learn new word meanings. We can increase the number of new words children learn from our teacher read-aloud by choosing some books specifically for their vocabulary development potential. For young children, alphabet books with just a few words and clear illustrations for each word can greatly increase the size of children's vocabularies while simultaneously teaching them important letter-name, letter-sound, and phonemic awareness concepts. There are many wonderful alphabet books. Here are some of my favorites, with examples of the vocabulary concepts built by the clear and clever illustrations:

John Burningham's ABC by John Burningham
clown; elephant; iguana; jungle; lion; mice; king; queen; tractor; volcano

A Is for Astronaut by Sian Tucker
bucket; envelope; frog; gloves; helicopter; kangaroo; ladybug; pear; rainbow

A to Z Sticker Book by Jan Pienkowski
alligators; bull; dolphins; koala; nurse; parachute; zigzag

The Timbertoes ABC by Highlights for Children
ant; castle; goat; ladder; mushroom; picnic; quilt; raft; wagon; yarn

The Accidental Zucchini by Max Grover
canyon; elevator; goldfish; railroad; sailor; tuba; yard

In addition to alphabet books, simple and clearly illustrated concept books help children add words and meanings to their vocabularies. Here are a few of the many wonderfully illustrated concept books:

Roger Priddy has a whole series of concept books including *Opposites; Colors; Shapes;* and *My Big World.*

Children love the Richard Scarry books including *Cars and Trucks; Things that Go; A Day at the Airport;* and *A Day at the Fire Station.*

Sandra Boynton is another author of concept books including *Horns to Toes; One, Two, Three!;* and *The Going to Bed Book.*

With both alphabet books and concept books, it is important to read the books to the children several times. On the first reading, read the book and encourage the children to talk about what they see in the pictures. On the second reading, have children predict what pictures and words they will see before turning to each page. To get more children speaking more words, seat your children in "talking partners" and ask them to talk with their partners.

Before you turn each page, they can tell their partners what they think will be on that page. After you read a page, ask them to talk with their partners about their experience with the words pictured. For example, you might say, "Talk to your partner about what you do on a rainy day when you are at home."

In addition to choosing some books to read aloud specifically for their vocabulary development potential, vocabulary growth can be accelerated by focusing on some vocabulary words in anything you read to your students. Several studies have demonstrated the power of focused read-alouds on fostering vocabulary growth (Beck, McKeown, & Kucan, 2002; Juel, Biancarosa, Coker, & Deffes, 2003). In each study, teachers went beyond just reading books aloud to children. Before they read the books aloud, they selected a few words that they felt many children would not know the meanings of. After the book had been read aloud and discussed, teachers returned to those selected words and focused student attention on them.

To maximize vocabulary growth from reading, many teachers choose one piece each week and use that book, magazine, or newspaper article to teach

Accelerating Vocabulary Growth for English Language Learners

Including clearly illustrated alphabet and concept books in your teacher read-aloud will increase the meaning vocabularies for all your students but it is crucial for your English language learners. Most children who are learning English have the concepts illustrated in these books—they just don't know the English word that goes with the concept. Have your ELLs tell their talking partner what the word in their first language is for the various pictures. Be sure to assign your ELLs an empathetic talking partner who will support and encourage them as they attempt to use the English words. Using the new words in speech is important for all children to learn new words but speaking the words is essential for children learning English. Alphabet and simple concept books are appropriate read-alouds for all young children including ELLs. These same books are a wonderful source for vocabulary development if you teach older children who are just beginning to learn English.

their students how to learn new words from the reading. This procedure is called "Three Read-Aloud Words" and here is how each lesson is carried out:

1. **Identify three "Goldilocks" words from a piece you are going to read aloud.**

   Any good book or article is going to have many words on which you could focus your attention. Narrowing the number of words you are going to teach to a reasonable number increases the chances that all your children will learn them. Beck, McKeown, and Kucan (2002) divided vocabulary into three tiers. The first tier includes words generally known by almost all children. *Boy*, *girl*, *jump*, *sad*, *laugh*, and *late* are examples of Tier 1 words. Many of your students will not know Tier 2 words but will need to know them. *Despair*, *exhausted*, *catastrophe*, and *proceeded* are Tier 2 words. Tier 3 words include uncommon, obscure, and technical words. *Languid*, *thrush*, *oblique*, and *catamaran* are examples of Tier 3 words. Beck and other experts suggest that we focus our time and energy in vocabulary development in teaching Tier 2 words. Some people refer to the Tier 2 words as "Goldilocks" words because they are not too well known, not too obscure, but hopefully "just right" for your students.

   As you begin to select your three Goldilocks words from the piece you are going to read aloud to your students, you will probably find a lot more than three possibilities. Narrow it down to three by considering the usefulness and appeal of the words to your children and how well the words are defined by the context and pictures. You might also choose a word because it has a word part (prefix, suffix, or root) you want your students to notice and analyze.

   If you have more than three words that are useful, appealing, and well defined, consider how many times each word occurs in the text. Your best choices should be central to the text and occur many times. Once you have chosen the three words, write them on index cards. For this example lesson, we are going to imagine that you have chosen an article from *Sports Illustrated for Kids* and the three words you chose to focus on are *overpowered*, *resurgent*, and *squandered*.

2. **Read the text the first time, making no reference to the three chosen words.**

   The first time you read anything aloud should always be for enjoyment and information. Read the piece to your children as you normally would, stopping from time to time to ask questions that will engage your students in the text but without doing anything particular about your chosen words.

3. Show the three words to your students.

After reading and enjoying the piece, show your students the words on index cards, one at a time. Have your students pronounce the words but do *not* let anyone share any meanings. This may feel quite counterintuitive. As teachers, we are used to giving students meanings for words or asking them for meanings they know. However, when doing Three Read-Aloud Words, you want your students to discover that they can learn new words from their reading by thinking about the context along with any pictures or known word parts. If you let anyone tell what a word means, you have defeated your purpose of demonstrating how the students can acquire new meanings from their reading. If one of your students responds to a word by saying, "I know what *overpowered* means," your response should be, "I am so glad you think you know but wait to tell us until we get to *overpowered* in the article!"

4. Reread the text and have the children stop you when you read each of the words.

Put the index cards with your three chosen words where your children can clearly see them. Now read the text to them again. On this second reading, do not stop to discuss pictures or engage the children with questions. When you come to one of the chosen words, some of your children are sure to notice and signal you. Tell students to stop you by shouting "STOP" and the word (for example, "Stop! *Overpowered*!"). No hand raising allowed in this activity!

When they signal you, stop reading and use the context, pictures, and word parts to explain each word. If words are repeated more than once, let the children stop you each time and see if any new information is added to their understanding of the word. Here is an example of the context in which each word occurs and how to model figuring out the meaning of each word.

> Abreu and Rodriguez each scored four times and Hideki Matsui hit a two-run double, helping the **resurgent** Yankees set a season high for runs in winning for the ninth time in 11 games. It's their longest winning streak since they won six straight last September. (*Sports Illustrated for Kids*, June 11, 2007, p. 2)

For **resurgent**, use the context—"winning for the ninth time in 11 games . . . longest winning streak"—along with the meanings of word parts the children know—**re** and **surge**—and conclude that the word **resurgent** means "coming back."

Alex Rodriguez homered twice and drove in five runs, Bobby Abreu went 4-for-4 with three RBIs and the Yankees **overpowered** Pittsburgh for their sixth consecutive victory. (*Sports Illustrated for Kids*, June 11, 2007, p. 2)

For **overpowered**, again use the context and the meanings of word parts—**over** and **power**—to determine that **overpowered** means won the game by being much stronger.

Clippard quickly **squandered** the lead. He walked two in the fourth and gave up a two-run double to No. 9 batter Chris Duffy, followed by José Bautista's two-run single off the left-field fence that put Pittsburgh up 6–5. (*Sports Illustrated for Kids*, June 11, 2007, p. 2)

Squandered has no word parts to help, but the children conclude from the context that Clippard's team was in the lead but gave it up by walking two batters and then letting the next two players get hits. **Squandered** means wasted, lost, or gave up.

5. **Help the children connect their own experience to the three words.**

   Once you have finished reading the book, stopping each time one of the chosen words occurs, focus again on each word and ask a question that helps children connect their own experience to the text. For these words, you might ask students

   "Can you think of a time when a team you were on or a favorite team was resurgent?"

   "Have you or a favorite player ever overpowered someone or been overpowered by someone?"

   "What could you squander in addition to the lead in a game?"

Let students turn and talk with each other for a minute after you ask each question. Then let them share their connections with these three words.

6. **Reread and have the children retell, using the three words in their retelling.**

   On the next day, after the first and second readings of the text, show the children the words once more and tell them that you are going to read the book, story, or magazine article to them one more time. This time they are to listen to everything that happens in the text—paying special attention to the order in which things happen and to the three words. Seat your children in "talking partners" and tell them that after you read, they will try to retell the information to their partner and use the three words in their retelling. Reread the piece, without stopping. As soon as you finish, ask your students to turn to their partner and retell the information using the three words, *resurgent*, *overpowered*, and *squandered*, in their retelling.

7. **Display the title and the three word cards somewhere in the room.**

    After you have introduced these three words and modeled for the children how context, pictures, and word parts are helpful in figuring out meanings for new words, assisted the children in connecting these words to their own experiences, and given them an opportunity to use these words to retell the text, display these words someplace in the room. You may want to copy the article or cover of the book and display the three index cards next to it. Tell your students that you and they are going to be on the lookout for these words in

Read-Aloud Words Posters

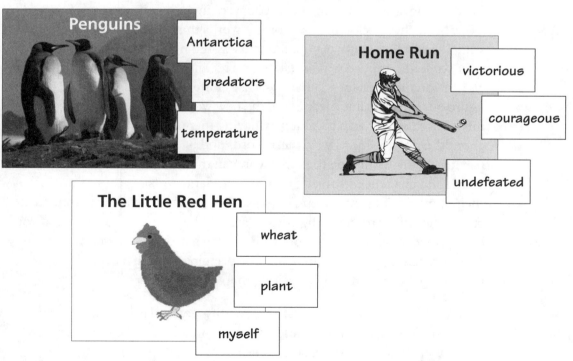

books and conversations and to try to use the words at school and at home. Every time someone hears, reads, or uses one of these words, he or she can put a tally mark next to the word. The word with the most tally marks at the end of one week is the winning word! (Kids love competitions, especially if they cannot possibly be the loser!) Once you do this, contrive to use these words in your conversations with the children over the next several days. Congratulate them when they notice the word and allow them to put a tally mark next to the word. Soon, you will notice that the students are trying to sneak these words into their talk—exactly what you are aiming for! Once the children are alert to these words, ask them to listen for the words and to try to use them in their home environments. Let the children report any instances of these words in their home environments and add tally marks to the appropriate words.

Three Read-Aloud Words Maximizes Vocabulary Growth through Reading

Imagine that every week throughout the school year you used the Three Read-Aloud strategy for one piece you were including in your teacher read-aloud. You chose "Goldilocks" words—words that would be useful to your students and that many of your students would not have meanings for. When your students stopped you in the second reading when they heard one of the words, you modeled for them how to use context, pictures, and word parts to figure out the probable meaning of the new word. You gave them an opportunity to use the words in speaking by having them "turn and talk" to a partner about their connections with these words and by having them retell with a partner, trying to include the three words in their retelling. You displayed the words and challenged yourself and your students to "slip" these words into their conversations. At the end of the school year, what have you done to increase the children's meaning vocabularies? The obvious answer is that you have provided direct instruction, with approximately 100 words. In providing that instruction, you have implemented principles for effective vocabulary instruction described in the previous chapter:

- Pictures and other visuals help solidify word meanings. (This example did not have picture clues but there would be picture clues for words you chose from other selections.)

- To truly own a word, children must use that word in speaking and writing. (Writing was not included but several different speaking opportunities were provided.)
- A set of essential words should be directly taught.
- Because most new words are learned through reading, teacher read-aloud and independent reading time should be scheduled into every elementary student's day.
- Students should be taught strategies for learning new words independently from reading, including instruction in word parts, context, and effective use of the dictionary.

Although teaching these 100 words in a maximally effective way is a worthwhile achievement, the most important thing you have accomplished is not the teaching of these 100 words. If you implement the Three Read-Aloud Words strategy every week, you will have modeled many times how you can learn new words from your reading. This brings to mind the old expression about giving a hungry person a fish versus teaching that person how to fish. Three Read-Aloud Words does give your students words; more importantly, it empowers all your students to grow their own vocabularies as they engage in their own reading.

Make Independent Reading an Everyday Event

The goal of every elementary teacher should be to have all children reading for at least 20 minutes each day from materials they have chosen to read. Use an analogy to help your children understand that becoming good at reading is just like becoming good at anything else. Compare learning to read with learning to play the piano, tennis, or baseball. Explain that in order to become good at anything, you need three things: (1) instruction, (2) practice on the skills, and (3) practice on the whole thing. To become a good tennis player, you need to (1) take tennis lessons, (2) practice the skills (backhand, serve, etc.), and (3) play tennis. To become a good reader, you also need instruction, practice on the important skills, and practice reading! Point out that sometimes we get so busy that we may forget to take the important time each day to read and therefore we must schedule it just like anything else we do.

Although at least 20 minutes daily for independent reading is the goal, most teachers start with a shorter period of time and increase the time gradually as children establish the reading habit and learn to look forward to this daily "read what you want to" time. Some teachers use a timer to signal the beginning and end of the independent reading time. When we engage in activities regularly, we establish some natural time rhythms. Using a timer to monitor the independent reading time helps children establish these rhythms. When the timer sounds at the end of the session, you should probably say something like, "Take another minute if you need to get to a stopping point."

Once the time for independent reading begins, do not allow the children to move around the room looking for something to read. Some teachers have children choose several pieces of reading material before the time begins and do not allow children to get up and change material until the time ends. In other classrooms, a crate of books is placed on each table and the children choose from that crate. The book crates rotate from table to table so that all the children have access to lots of different books "within arm's length."

Establishing and enforcing the "no wandering" rule is particularly important for struggling readers. If children have not been successful with reading in the past and they are allowed to move around the room to look for books during the independent reading time, they are very apt to spend more time wandering than reading. Remember that one of your major reasons for committing yourself to this daily independent reading time is that you know that how much the children read plays a critical role in how well they read. If your good readers read for almost all the allotted time and your struggling readers read for only half the time, the gap between your good and poor readers will further widen as the year goes on. Having a good variety of materials "within arm's reach" is crucial if struggling readers are going to profit from this precious time you are setting aside each day for independent reading.

If you begin with just five or six minutes, kindergartners and early first-graders can engage in independent reading even before they can read. Think about your own children or young children you have known. Young children who have been read to regularly often look at their books and pretend they are reading. Kindergartners and early first-graders should be encouraged to get in the habit of reading even before they can do it. Many teachers of young children prompt with "Pretend that you are the teacher and you are reading the book." Kindergarten children are also very motivated to read if they are allowed to select a stuffed animal or a doll to read to!

Accumulate the Widest Possible Variety of Reading Materials

To have successful independent reading, it is crucial that students choose their own reading materials and have a variety of materials from which to choose. Collecting lots of appealing books requires determination, cleverness, and an eye for bargains. In addition to obvious sources such as free books you get from book clubs when your students order books, asking parents to donate, begging for books from your friends and relatives whose children have outgrown them, and haunting yard sales and thrift shops, there are some less obvious sources as well. Libraries often sell or donate used books and magazines on a regular basis. Some bookstores will give you a good deal on closeouts and may even set up a "donation basket" where they will collect used books for you. (Take some pictures of your eager readers and have your children write letters telling what kind of books they like to read for the store to display above the donation basket.)

Many classrooms subscribe to some of the popular children's magazines. You will have far fewer resistant readers if the latest issue and back copies of *Jack and Jill*, *Children's Digest*, *Cricket*, *Soccer Junior*, *Ranger Rick*, *3-2-1 Contact*, *Sports Illustrated for Kids*, *National Geographic for Kids*, and *Zoobooks* are available for children to read during independent reading time.

Another inexpensive source of motivating reading materials are the news magazines for children, including *Scholastic News*, *Weekly Reader*, and *Time for Kids*. They generally cost about $4.00 per copy and you get a "desk copy" with orders of 10 to 12 copies. Teachers across a grade level often share the magazines, with each classroom receiving 2 or 3 copies. These news magazines deal with topics of real interest to kids, and reading interest is always heightened on the day that a new issue arrives.

Be sure you make the materials you read aloud to your students available for them to read. Wanting to read the book the teacher read is one of the major reasons children give for choosing particular books. And don't forget to read aloud some easy books (called "everyone" books) so that all children can read on their own some of the books you read to them. Including concept and alphabet books in your teacher read-aloud and reading them aloud to the children several times will ensure that even your most struggling readers can feel successful during the independent reading time.

Schedule Conferences So You Can Talk with Children about Their Reading

Early in the year when you are getting your students in the habit of reading every day and gradually increasing the time for independent reading, circulate around and have whispered conversations with individual children about their books. Once the independent reading time is well established, schedule conferences with four or five students each day. Use this time to monitor each child's reading, to encourage the children in their individual reading interests, and to help children with book selection if needed.

If your reading conferences are going to be something your students look forward to (instead of dreading!), you need to think of them as conversations rather than interrogations. Here are some "conference starters" you might use to set a positive and encouraging tone for reading conferences:

"Let's see, what have you got for me today?"

"Oh good, another book about ocean animals. I had no idea there were so many books about ocean animals!"

"I see you have bookmarked two pages to share with me. Read these pages to me and tell me why you chose them."

"I never knew there was so much to learn about animals in the ocean. I am so glad you bring such interesting books to share with me each week. You are turning me into an ocean animals expert!"

"I can't wait to see what you bring to share with me next week!"

One trick to make sure your conferences are "kid-centered" conversations rather than interrogations is to put the job of preparing for the conference on the child. Before you begin conferences, use modeling and role-playing to help the children learn what their job is in the conference. The children choose the book (or magazine) they want to share and bookmark the part they want to share. Make sure your students know that since you will only have 3 or 4 minutes with each student, they must prepare and be ready for the conference. After role-playing and modeling, many teachers post a chart to remind children what they are to do on the day of their conference.

Getting Ready for Your Reading Conference

1. Pick the book or magazine you want to share.

2. Choose a part to read to me and practice this part.

3. Write the title and page number on a bookmark and put the bookmark in the right place.

4. Think about what you want to talk to me about. Some possibilities are:

   What you like about this book.

   Why you chose this part to read to me.

   Other good parts of the book.

   What you think will happen (if you haven't finished the book).

   What you are thinking about sharing with me next week.

   Who you think would also like this book.

Rather than arbitrarily assigning one-fifth of the class to the different conference days, many teachers divide up their struggling and most advanced readers across the days. The first child listed on each day is one of the five most struggling readers. The second child is one of the most advanced readers.

Conference Schedule

Day 1	Day 2	Day 3	Day 4	Day 5
Todd	Marisol	Julio	Shandra	Ian
Carla	Belinda	Tyrone	Tracy	Christine
Patrice	Carlos	Vincent	Tiffany	Mike
Tony	Antoine	Elizabeth	Richard	Sandy
Alex	Michael	Trisha	Matt	Juan

Teachers often spend an extra minute with the struggling reader scheduled for the day. Struggling readers often need help selecting books they can read, and after the child shares the book chosen for that day, the teacher may want to help the child select some books he or she might want to read next week. Advanced readers might also need an extra minute to help with book selection. These excellent readers often read books that are too easy for them. Certainly, reading easy books is good for everyone, but it is nice for the teacher to have a minute to nudge them forward in their book selection. Clever teachers do this in a "seductive" rather than a heavy-handed way:

> "Carla, I know you love mysteries, and the other day when I was in the library I found two mysteries that made me think of you. Listen to this." (Teacher reads "blurb" on the back of each mystery to Carla.) "Now, I have to warn you. These mysteries are a little longer and harder than the ones you usually read but you are such a good reader, I know you could handle them if you wanted to read them."

Carla is probably delighted that the teacher thought of her and thinks she could read harder mysteries and will very likely "take the bait" and go off with some mysteries closer to her advanced reading level.

Students who read books they *want* to read motivates them to read more. Sharing those books once a week with someone who "oohs and aahs" about their reading choices is also a sure-fire motivator.

Make Time for Sharing and Responding

Children who read also enjoy talking to their classmates about what they have read. In fact, Manning and Manning (1984) found that providing time for children to interact with one another about reading material enhanced the effects of sustained silent reading on both reading achievement and attitudes. One device sure to spark conversation about books is to create a classroom bookboard. Cover a bulletin board with white paper and use yarn to divide it into 40 to 50 spaces. Select 40 to 50 titles from the classroom library and write each title in one of the spaces. Next, make some small construction paper rectangles in three colors or use three colors of small sticky notes. Designate a color to stand for various reactions to the books, such as:

- Red indicates "Super—one of the all-time best books I've ever read."
- Blue indicates "OK—not the best book I've ever read but still enjoyable."
- Yellow indicates "Yucky, boring—a waste of time!"

Children are encouraged to read as many of the bookboard books as possible and to put their "autograph" on a red, blue, or yellow rectangle and attach it to the appropriate title. Once a week, the teacher leads the class in a lively discussion of the reasons for their book evaluations. Some books will be universally declared "reds," "blues," or "yellows," but other books will collect evaluations in all three colors. As the weeks go on, most everyone will want to read the red books and some will choose the yellow books to see if they really are that bad. After most children have read these books, begin a new bookboard. This time, allow each child to select a book title or two to put on the bookboard and to label/decorate the spot for that book.

In some classrooms the self-selected block ends with a Reader's Chair in which one or two children each day get to do a book talk. They show a favorite book and read or tell a little about the book and then try to "sell" the book to the rest of the class. Their selling techniques appear to be quite effective, since these books are usually quickly seen in the hands of many of their classmates.

Other teachers have "reading parties" one afternoon every two or three weeks. Children's names are pulled from a jar and they form a group of three or four in which everyone gets to share their favorite book. Reading parties, like other parties, often include refreshments such as popcorn or cookies. Children develop all kinds of tasty associations with books and sharing books!

Finding time for children to talk about books is not easy in today's crowded curriculum. There is, however, a part of each day that is not well used in most elementary classrooms—the last 15 minutes of the day. Many teachers have found that they can successfully schedule weekly reading sharing time if they utilize those last 15 minutes. Here is an example of how this sharing time works in one classroom.

Every Thursday afternoon, the teacher gets the children completely ready to be dismissed 15 minutes before the final bell rings. Notes to go home are distributed. Bookbags are packed. Chairs are placed on top of the desks. The teacher then uses index cards and writes down each child's name on a card. The index cards are shuffled and the first five names—which will form the first group—are called. These children go to a corner of the room that will always be the meeting place for the first group. The next five names that come out will form the second group and will go to whichever place is designated for the second group. The process continues until all five or six groups are formed and the children are in their places. Now, each child has two minutes to read, tell, show, act out, or otherwise share something from what she or he has been reading this week. The children share in the order that their names were called. The first person called for each group is the leader. Each person has exactly two minutes and is timed by a timer. When the timer sounds, the next person gets two minutes. If a few minutes remain after all the children have had their allotted two minutes, the leader of each group selects something to share with the whole class.

Teachers who have used such a procedure to ensure that children have a chance to talk with others about what they read on a regular basis find that the children are more enthusiastic about reading. Comments such as "I'm going to stump them with these riddles when I get my two minutes," and "Wait 'til I read the scary part to everyone," are proof that sharing helps motivate reading. The popularity of the books shared with other children is further proof. Having discussions on a specified afternoon each week puts this procedure on the schedule and ensures that it will get done. Using the cards to form the groups is quick and easy and helps ensure that children will interact with many other children over the course of the year.

✿ Alert Children to New Words They Meet in Their Reading

If you are doing the Three Read-Aloud Words and taking your students on "Picture Walks" before reading, you are already doing a lot to help children be alert to new words in their own reading. Your students will be in the habit of looking at the pictures and thinking about what words in the text these pictures relate to. They will know how the context of what you are reading often makes clear the meaning of a word and that each time you meet the same word, the additional context often adds to or clarifies your meaning for that word. If you want to give them an additional nudge, however, to use what they know about learning word meanings from their reading, designate one day each week as a "Sticky Note Day." At the beginning of their independent reading time, give each child one sticky note. Ask the child to be on the lookout for one word that is relatively new to him or her and that the child can figure out the meaning of based on the context and the pictures. Explain to the students how you choose your Three Read-Aloud Words by looking for words that many of them don't know but that are useful and interesting words. Tell the children that you also try to choose words where the context and pictures make the meaning clear and that are used more than once.

Ask your students to be on the lookout during their reading for a perfect word to teach to the class. They should write that word on a sticky note and place the sticky note on the sentence in which they first see the word. When the time for independent reading is over, gather your students together and let four or five volunteers tell their word and read the context and/or share the picture that helped them with the meaning of that word. Do not let all your children share their words, because this would take more time than you have, and you want your students to be excited about finding new words—not bored with having to listen to 25 explanations! Assure your students that you will give them another sticky note next Thursday and that you will let other children share their findings with the class.

Example of "Sticky Note" Sentence

The ozone layer forms a thin shield high up in the sky. It protects life on Earth from the sun's ultraviolet (UV) rays. In the 1980s, scientists began finding clues that the ozone layer was going away or being depleted. This allows more UV radiation to reach the surface. This can cause people to have a greater chance of getting too much UV radiation. UV can cause bad health effects like skin damage, and get you sick easier.

depletion

If you designate one day each week as "Sticky Note New Word Day," your students will get in the habit of looking for interesting new words and using the pictures and context to figure out this word. Soon, they will be doing this in all their reading—even when they don't have a blank sticky note staring at them—and they will be on their way to adding exponentially to their vocabularies every time they read!

Another simple way to keep students alert for new words is to designate some space in your room as a "Vocabulary Board." Supply your students with lots of colorful index cards and markers and encourage them to add new words they find in their reading to the board. They should initial the card on which they write the word so everyone can tell who found which words. Take a few minutes each day to note new additions to the vocabulary board and ask students where they found the word, what it means, and why they thought everyone would want to learn that word.

Maximize Vocabulary Growth through Teacher Read-Aloud and Independent Reading

In today's crowded curriculum with so much emphasis on standards and tests, some teachers feel they can no longer afford the luxury of taking time out every day to read to their students and providing time every day for students to develop the reading habit as they engage in independent reading. When you consider that most new words students add to their vocabularies were probably encountered during reading, the decision to eliminate these time-tested activities seems very short-sighted. The size of your students' meaning vocabulary is the biggest determinant of comprehension. Children who read more have larger vocabularies. Your students will read more if you regularly read aloud to your students, provide time for independent reading, and encourage the children to share their reading with each other. Add some direct instruction on how to learn new words from reading, and you can maximize the potential of your teacher read-aloud and independent reading. When you think about vocabulary development, teacher read-aloud and independent reading are not luxuries—they are necessities!

chapter 3

Maximizing Vocabulary Development by Teaching Word Parts

English is one of the most morphologically complex languages. For every word we know, there are six or seven other words we can attach meaning to if we are "morphologically sophisticated."

Morphology refers to word parts—roots, prefixes, and suffixes—that add meanings to words or change their grammatical function. Linguists estimate that about half of all new words we encounter are structurally related to other words (Anglin, 1993). Read this fictionalized account of a high school baseball game and think about why certain words are shaded and other words have a part bolded at the beginning or end of the word.

Underdogs Win Champion**ship**

Yesterday afternoon, Smithtown made the district playoffs by winning both games of a doubleheader against Parkwood. The games were played at the new County Ballpark under a cloud**less** sky. In the first game, Smithtown coach Jose Martinez started the Bobcats' best pitch**er**, Ivey Hanes. Hanes used his fastball and slid**er** to shutout the Parkwood hitt**er**s for the first five innings. Meanwhile, the Bobcats' hitt**er**s scored three runs off the Grasshoppers' start**er**, Jock Jackson. In the first inning, Jackson's screwball and changeup looked **un**hitt**able** until Smithtown's catch**er**, Chi Park, hit an **in**cred**ible** home run over the scoreboard in right field. In the fourth inning, Jackson got two quick outs but then could not find the strike zone. He loaded the bases with Bobcat runn**er**s and walked the next batt**er** in for an **un**earned run. Hanes batted in the Bobcats' third run with a sacrifice fly to a Parkwood outfield**er** that brought Eric Price home from third base. After that, Jackson **re**covered his concentration and **over**powered the next Bobcat batt**er**. Jackson pitched hit**less** baseball after the fourth inning, but the damage was done. After the first game, Parkwood's coach, David Tyson, commented, "A shutout for our team was completely **un**expected. Even our best slugg**er**s struck out or hit ground**er**s. There was nothing I could do in our dugout but watch and weep!"

In the nightcap, Parkwood's starting pitch**er** was Juan Ortiz, fam**ous** for his power**ful** speedball. Smithtown countered with "Lucky" Brown, their freshman sensation, the youngest starting pitcher in Bobcat history. Brown allowed the Grasshopper shortstop, Mike Williamson, to reach base on a single. Parkwood's third baseman, Ryan Ford, hit a triple to score Williamson. During Brown's windup to the next batter, Ford stole home, making the score 2–0. In the fifth inning, the fireworks started with the play of the day. Bobcat infielder, Eric Price, hit a rainmaker off Ortiz. All three Grasshopper outfielders ran to catch the ball. The centerfielder, Keyshawn Upshaw, was closest to it when the ball seemed to disappear in the lights. After a few seconds of confusion, Upshaw located the ball in the air and leaped toward it, colliding with John Rice, Greenville's right fielder. The ball hit the ground and rolled to the outfield fence. Price scored his second run of the day on an "inside the park" home run, making the score 2–1. Then, the Bobcat catcher, Chi Park, hit a double off Ortiz. Coach Martinez sent in a pinch hitter for his next batter. Mark West, who had been a benchwarmer for the Bobcats all season, came through with a single that scored Park from second, making the score 2–2. West stole second base and then was driven home by Manuel Ho's long single, making the score 3–2 and giving Smithtown their first regular season championship in 22 years! After the game, Martinez said, "This just proves that an underdog like Smithtown can become the champion, if we play hard and don't give up."

What did you conclude about the shaded words? You probably noticed that all the shaded words are compound words. Compound words are made up of two root words. The meaning of the compound word combines the meanings of the two root words. Often the meaning of the compound word is quite obvious, even to the youngest reader. **Ballpark**, **outfield**, and **scoreboard** are examples of compound words with transparent meanings. Sometimes the meanings of compound words is not quite so obvious. It is clear what the **double** part of **doubleheader** refers to, but why is it called a **header**? Why would a certain kind of hit be called a **rainmaker**? Why would a player be called a **benchwarmer**? Compound words abound in English and are particularly common in sports terminology. In addition to sports-specific compound words, this newspaper article, like most text, contains compound words with more general meaning such as **afternoon**, **meanwhile**, **fireworks**, and **freshman**.

Now think about the words that have some bolded letters at the beginning: **un**hittable, **un**earned, **un**expected, **in**credible, **dis**appear, **re**covered, **over**powered, and **under**dog. These words all have root words with another word part, prefixes added to the beginning of the word. As with compound words, sometimes the meaning of the prefixed word is transparent if you know the meaning of the root word and the prefix. The most common prefix, **un**, appears three times in this article. In all three words—**un**hittable, **un**earned, and **un**expected—**un** turns the root word into the opposite. The next three most common prefixes—**re**, **in**, and **dis**—are found in the words **re**covered, **in**credible, and **dis**appeared. Also, **under** and **over** are common prefixes and occur here in the words **under**dog and **over**powered.

This article also includes many words with suffixes. **Er**, meaning a person who does the action, is a very common suffix that occurs in many words, including pitch**er**, catch**er**, batt**er**, hitt**er**, start**er**, runn**er**s, slugg**er**s, benchwarm**er**, infield**er**, outfield**er**, and centerfield**er**. The suffix **er** can also refer to a thing that does something, shown here by the words slid**er** and ground**er**. **Est**, meaning **most**, is another common suffix and is represented here by young**est** and clos**est**. **Less** and **ful** are two other suffixes that change the meaning of words. This article contains the words cloud**less**, hit**less**, and power**ful**. Some suffixes don't change the meaning of a word but do change its grammatical function. **Able**, **ible**, **ous**, **sion**, and **ship** are examples of grammatical suffixes and occur in the words unhitt**able**, incred**ible**, fam**ous**, confu**sion**, and champion**ship.**

There is another very common type of suffix called an inflectional suffix and this suffix does not change meaning or grammatical function. **S**, **ed**, and **ing** are inflectional suffixes and occur in numerous words in everything we read, including champion**s**, leap**ed**, and collid**ing**.

The previous chapter described how important context and pictures are to independently learning word meanings. In reality, morphology (word parts) and information gained from context and pictures are used together to figure out the new words. Imagine that before reading the baseball article, you were totally unfamiliar with the word **benchwarmer**. The first time you ever see or hear **benchwarmer**, it is in this context.

> Coach Martinez sent in a pinch hitter for his next batter. Mark West, who had been a benchwarmer for the Bobcats all season, came through with a single that scored Park from second, making the score 2–2.

From the context, you figure out that the **benchwarmer** is one of the Bobcat players. Because he is a pinch hitter, you know he is not a regular starter. But why is he called a **benchwarmer**? Putting together the meanings of the two roots—**bench** and **warm**—and adding **er** (the person who does the action), you figure out that he must sit on the bench a lot during games and you realize that **benchwarmer** is a clever way of describing a player who doesn't play much and thus "warms the bench!"

Elementary students add a huge number of words to their meaning vocabularies each year. Some of these words are directly taught by their teachers. The majority of the words, however, are gained through wide reading. To maximize the number of words students learn from their reading, we must teach students how to use context and pictures, and we must teach them word parts, and how to combine them with context to infer meanings for new words. The problem is that instruction in word parts is not generally very engaging or motivating—for teachers or students. Sports, however, are of universal interest to students.

This chapter will suggest activities that teach students to use word parts, and the "hook" for some of that instruction will be sports articles found in your local newspaper! Of course, you can use any other reading materials for your word-part instruction. Just be sure the material you are using is of high interest and motivating for your students.

✿ Begin with Compound Words

Your goal in all morphology instruction is to get your students into the habit of looking at an unfamiliar word and asking the question: "Do I know any of the word parts?" Because compound words abound in English and because figuring out the meaning of a compound word by thinking about the meanings of the two words that make up the compound is a relatively easy task, begin your word-part instruction with compound words. Find an article in your local newspaper or in *Sports Illustrated for Kids* that has several compound words and read that article to your students. For the first reading, don't focus on the compound words but only on the content of the article and what happened in the game. Choose an article about a team your kids care about and, if possible, one in which the favorite team wins! Next, reread the article and this time ask your students to stop you when they hear a compound word. Use the Three Read-Aloud Words procedure described in Chapter 2 but have students stop you by shouting, "Stop—*Compound*!"

After stopping for each compound word, write that word on the board and ask students to tell you the two words making up the compound and how these words add to the meaning of the compound word. Just as in our example, the meaning of some compounds will be familiar—such as **football**, **kickoff**, **touchdown**. Other words may be less familiar and the meaning of the words that make up the compound less obvious—for example **shotgun** and **touchback**—and students may need to use the context of the article to infer the word meanings.

Next, put students in groups and give each group the sports section of the newspaper and a highlighter. Give them 12 minutes to find and highlight as many compound words as they can. When the time is up, let the groups share the words and explain what each means using prior knowledge and/or context.

Begin a compound bulletin board by having each group divide up the task of writing the compound words on large index cards. Students should write the compound word on one side of the card in large letters with a marker. On the back of the card, have them write the sentence in which they found the word. While the groups work on this task, write the compound words from the article you read to them along with sentences on the back on index cards. Attach all words to a compound bulletin board. Tell the students that for the next two weeks, everyone will be searching for compound words in everything they read. Provide lots of index cards and colorful markers. Ask students to "initial" and date each card before attaching it to the board so that everyone will know who found the word. Be sure to include some words you find during your teacher read-aloud. Take a few minutes each day to see what compound words were added to the collection. By the end of the two weeks,

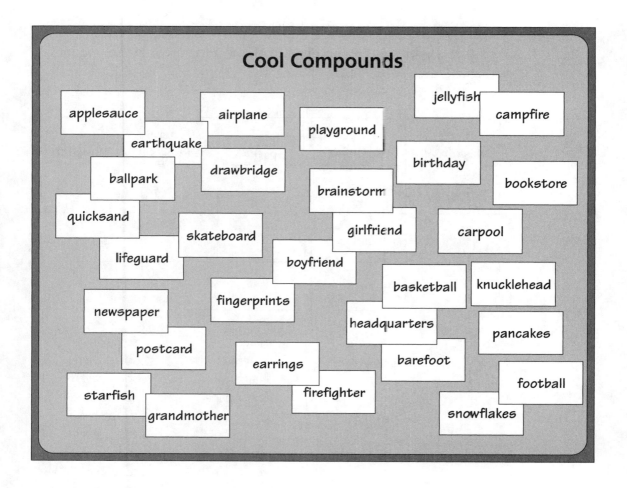

Cool Compounds

applesauce · airplane · playground · jellyfish · campfire · earthquake · drawbridge · birthday · ballpark · brainstorm · bookstore · quicksand · skateboard · girlfriend · carpool · lifeguard · boyfriend · basketball · knucklehead · newspaper · fingerprints · headquarters · pancakes · postcard · earrings · barefoot · football · starfish · firefighter · snowflakes · grandmother

the compound board will look like a "collage" with new words on top of older ones. Don't worry if your compound board is crowded and messy. You have accomplished your goal of alerting your students to the pervasiveness of compound words and how they can learn new words by thinking about the meanings of the words making up the compounds and the context. You have also launched your students successfully on their word-part journey!

Compound Sort

While on the hunt for compounds you may also want to provide more practice with compounds by having your students do a compound word sort. Put your students in groups and give them a list of compound words and some categories to sort for. Have the group decide in which category each word belongs and write it in the appropriate column. Here are some compound words that can be sorted into six categories.

Football	Basketball	Baseball/ Softball	Soccer	General Sports	Nonsports

afternoon	dugout	linebacker	somewhat
airplane	earring	lineman	somewhere
airport	earthquake	nationwide	southpaw
anyone	everybody	newspaper	speedball
anywhere	everywhere	nightcap	sweatshirt
backdoor	fastball	notebook	teammates
backstop	fingernails	offside	thunderstorm
ballpark	football	outcome	touchback
baseline	fullback	outfield	touchdown
baseman	goalkeeper	overtime	touchline
benchwarmer	goalpost	playground	turnpike
birthday	goaltending	quarterback	underdog
bookstore	goldfish	rainmaker	underhand
carpool	grandmother	scoreboard	upstairs
changeup	haircut	screwball	whatever
classmate	halfback	shootout	windup
cornerback	headache	shortstop	workshop
crossover	headlights	shotgun	wraparound
crosswalk	homework	shutout	yourself
daylight	infield	sidearm	
doubleheader	kickoff	sideline	
downtown	lifeguard	somehow	

Writing Compounds

In Chapter 1, several principles for vocabulary development were stated. One of these principles was:

> To truly own a word, children must use that word in speaking and writing.

The major reason for putting students in groups to find and sort compound words is so they would talk to one another about these words, which helps you accomplish the speaking goal. Once you begin collecting compounds, do some "quick-writes" in which students use the compound board and any compound word sort to write something, trying to "sneak in" as many compound words as they can. Model for the students that their writing can be silly by writing a few silly sentences yourself.

> The knuckleheads ate applesauce at the ballpark.
> The lifeguard saved his grandmother from the jellyfish.

Limit the time the students write to no more than 5 minutes and then let them share their silly sentences. Students usually enjoy this silly writing more if they are allowed to write with a friend if they choose.

❀ Prefixes

Four prefixes—**un**, **re**, **in**, and **dis**—are the most common and will help students figure out the meaning of over 1,500 words. Graves (2004) suggests teaching these prefixes to all elementary students. Teaching students to use prefixes and root words to add new words to their meaning vocabularies is important but it is more complicated than teaching them to use the parts of compound words. In many prefixed words, the meaning of the word is not easily figured out by simply combining the meaning of the prefix and the root. Often, words begin with syllables with the same spelling as prefixes but they are not prefixes. Knowing the opposite meaning of **im** helps you build meaning for **impatient** and **improbable** but not for **imagine** or **immense**. Students need to learn the common prefixes but they must also learn that not all words that begin like common prefixes will help them with the meaning of words.

The Prefix **un**

Because words that begin with the prefix **un** are the most common and because students know a lot of words in which the prefix **un** appears, prefix instruction should probably begin with words that begin with **un**. Begin your prefix instruction as you began your compound word instruction by reading something to your students that contains several **un** words. Use a high-interest newspaper or magazine article if you can find one that contains several **un** words or write a paragraph describing something your students have experienced, perhaps a recent loss of your students' favorite team.

On Friday night, East High's **unbeaten** football team was **unable** to score against Jonesboro High's **unmerciful** defense. With only 5 seconds left, Jonesboro's kicker **unloosed** a 40-yard field goal to win the game, 3–0. East High's head coach was **unrestrained** in his praise for Jonesboro's team. "Their defense was our **undoing**! I'm **uncertain** how many years it's been since we played a game and didn't score at least one touchdown. That's all we needed to win, but we were **unsuccessful** every time we got the ball. I'm also **unhappy** that we kept getting **untimely** penalties that stopped our progress or gave them good field position. We didn't lose because we were **unlucky**, but because we were **unworthy**!"

After reading the article the first time for meaning, have the students listen again and stop you when you come to any **un** words by shouting, "Stop! *Un*!" Each time they stop you, talk with them about the words and help them see that **un** often changes a word to its opposite meaning. Write these words on large index cards with the sentence on the back and use them for the beginning of your **un** bulletin board.

Next, put students in groups and have them brainstorm as many words as they can that begin with **un** and in which **un** turns the word into the opposite. Have students use markers to write the word on one side of the card and use pencil to write a sentence illustrating that word's meaning on the other side. When the time is up, let the groups share their words and use these cards to begin your **un** bulletin board.

Of course, you want students to hunt for **un** words as they did for compound words, but this hunt will be more complicated because in some words, **un** is not a prefix but only the first syllable. Using index cards of a different color, write several words in which **un** is not a prefix meaning the opposite—

for example, **uncle, understand,** and **uniform.** On the back of the card, write a sentence for each of these words. Attach these index cards to your **un** board and explain to students that they should use the white cards for words in which **un** turns a word into its opposite meaning and blue (or whatever color you have chosen) cards for any words they find that begin with **un** but in which **un** is not a prefix meaning "opposite" or "not." Just as with compound words, let the **un** collecting continue for two weeks and take a few minutes at the end of each day to talk about the new **un** words added and to read the sentences in which they were found. Model and remind students of this on-going hunt by adding some **un** words that occur during your teacher read-aloud, including some in which **un** is just a syllable and not a prefix meaning opposite. When your bulletin board is complete, have your students do some "silly writing" in which they have 5 minutes to use as many **un** words as they can. You may want to remind them of Alexander's terrible, horrible, no good, very bad day and suggest that they write about a bad day, real or imagined.

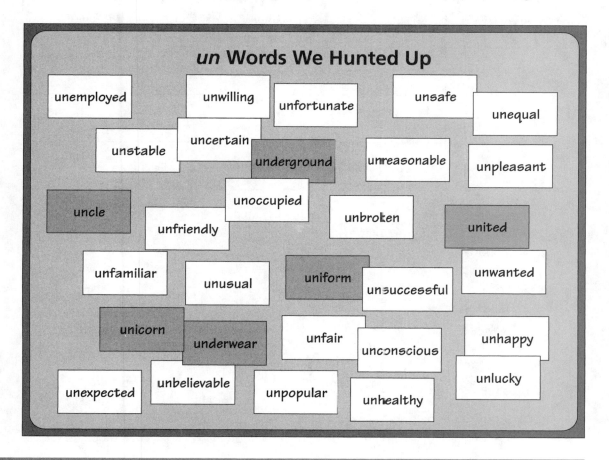

un Words We Hunted Up

unemployed · unwilling · unfortunate · unsafe · unequal · unstable · uncertain · underground · unreasonable · unpleasant · uncle · unoccupied · unfriendly · unbroken · united · unfamiliar · unusual · uniform · unsuccessful · unwanted · unicorn · underwear · unfair · unconscious · unhappy · unexpected · unbelievable · unpopular · unhealthy · unlucky

Prefixes **in** and **dis**

Two other prefixes, **in** and **dis**, are also fairly common and also have the meaning of "opposite" or "not." The complicating factor in teaching these prefixes is that there are many words in which the prefix does not have the opposite meaning or in which the opposite meaning would not be clear to your students. To further complicate matters, the prefix **in** is spelled **i-l** before words beginning with **l** (**illegal**, **illogical**), **i-r** before words beginning with **r** (**irrational**, **irreversible**), and **i-m** before words beginning with **p** (**impossible**, **impatient**). To teach these prefixes, students probably need to be given a list of words to sort, rather than coming up with words on their own. Here is a list of commonly known words and four categories into which students should work in groups to sort them.

dis Prefix Meaning "Not" or "Opposite"	*dis* Not a Prefix	*in/im/il/ir* Prefix Meaning "Not" or "Opposite"	*in/im/il/ir* Not a Prefix

distance	injury	impulsive	irregular
illegal	informal	disaster	discourage
innocent	disprove	immeasurable	important
discuss	illogical	include	disobey
dislike	incomplete	insane	impatient
illustration	discover	disorder	invitation
dispute	illiterate	inspire	disturbance
improve	impeach	independent	impossible
impure	incompetent	inexpensive	instrument
disgrace	discussion	disagree	incorrect
immigrant	impress	immortal	dishonest
distrust	disappear	inadequate	invite
increase	impostor	irrational	disappoint

illustrator	displeased	immediately	disappearance
irritation	improper	dissatisfied	disagreement
irresponsible	impossible	immigration	disloyal
imitate	disconnect	immune	discrimination
immobile	impartial	distributor	
irresistible	distasteful	disapproval	

Prefix **re**

Re, meaning "back" or "again," is another prefix that generates lots of words and that has many examples students know. Like **in** and **dis**, however, there are also a number of words that begin with **re** in which **re** is simply the first syllable and not a prefix. Put students in groups and have them sort **re** words into three categories.

re Prefix Meaning "Back"	*re* Prefix Meaning "Again"	*re* Not a Prefix

readjust	reelect	reopen	reread
reappear	refill	reorder	rerun
rearrange	refrigerator	reorganize	responsibility
rebound	refund	repaint	result
rebuild	refuse	repair	retire
recall	relax	repeat	return
receive	relay	replace	reunite
recess	relocate	replacement	review
recharge	remainder	replant	revolver
reconsider	remember	reply	reward
reconstruct	remodel	report	rewrite
recycle	remote	reporter	
reduce	rename	reproduce	

Less Common Prefixes

Un, **in**, **dis**, and **re** are clearly the prefixes that generate enough useful words to merit teaching to elementary students. Here are some other prefixes that occur much less often. These prefixes are probably not worth a whole lesson but it would be helpful to point them out to students when they occur during read-aloud or other lessons and alert students to their meaning. As with **un**, **dis**, **in**, and **re**, be sure students understand that not all words that begin with these letters will function as prefixes and help them with meaning.

in meaning "in"

inside   income   indent   indoors   infield   insight
intake   inland   inmate

mis meaning "wrong (wrongly)"

mistake   misbehave   misdeal   misjudge   mistrust
mistreat   misspell   misprint   misplace   mislead
misunderstood   misfortune

non meaning "not"

nonsense   nonliving   nonrenewable   nonexistent
nonessential   nonstop

pre meaning "before"

preview   pregame   prepay   pretest   precook   preexisting
preschool   preteen   preheat   premature

en meaning "make" or "put"

enjoy   enforce   enclose   ensure   enlarge   enrich
enlist   enable   encourage   enroll   enact   endanger
enrage   endear

over meaning "over" or "too much"

overpower   overdo   overcome   overwhelm   overjoyed
overhand   oversleep   overtime   overpass   overnight
overreact   overweight

under meaning "under" or "below"

underdog undergo underground underage
underhand underline underwear underestimate
underpass underweight underwater undercover

Just as with compound words, your purpose in teaching prefixes should be to help your students maximize the number of words they add to their vocabularies as they engage in reading throughout the day and across the curriculum. Your "big goal" is to help your students become morphologically sophisticated and to teach them that when they come to a big unknown word in their reading, they should ask themselves the key question: "Does this new word have any parts I know?" Students who combine the information provided by context and pictures with their knowledge of prefixes can add thousands of new words to their vocabularies.

Suffixes

Once students are in the habit of using the two words in a compound word and common prefixes to access word meanings, they can profit from instruction with the common suffixes. Most students easily learn the inflectional suffixes (also called endings) **s**, **es**, **ed**, and **ing** because they are so common in speech and writing. These endings do not change meaning or part of speech. Derivational suffixes, however, add meaning or change the grammatical function of the word. One complication with suffix instruction is that unlike parts of a compound word or prefixes, suffixes often require spelling and pronunciation changes. **Funny** becomes **funniest**, **beauty** becomes **beautiful**, and **sign** becomes **signature**. These changes not only make suffixes words difficult to spell but often result in young readers not recognizing the root word when a suffix is added. The most common and easy-to-understand suffixes that change meaning are **er** and **est** meaning "more" and "most," **er** meaning "person" or "thing that does something," **ful** and **less**, and **able/ible**. Because they are the most common and easiest to understand, suffix instruction should begin with these suffixes.

Teaching **er** and **est**

Because **er** and **est** are so common, you can probably find a newspaper sports article that contains a lot of **er** and **est** words. If not, write a short paragraph describing a sporting event your students care about. Use the previously described procedure of reading the article to your students for meaning first and then reading it again and asking students to stop you when they hear a word that ends in **er** meaning "more" or **est** meaning "most." As students stop you, write the word on an index card. If the word has a spelling change, be sure to point that out to your students and underline it on your index card.

Next, put your students in groups and let them hunt for words ending in **er** and **est** meaning "more" and "most." Students enjoy using highlighters to highlight these words. Once they have found and highlighted several words, have the group divide up the words and write them on index cards, underlining any spelling changes and writing the sentence in which they found them on the back. Use the index cards you made along with the ones made by your students to begin your **er/est** bulletin board and let students hunt for **er/est** meaning "more" and "most" words in everything they read and add these to the board.

Teaching **er** and Other Suffixes Meaning "Person" or "Thing"

The next common suffix that adds meaning to a word is **er** meaning "person" or "thing." Because this suffix is so common, you can probably use the now familiar procedure of reading something to your students and having them identify the **er** words and then letting groups of students find **er** words meaning "person" and "thing" and writing them on index cards to begin a bulletin board. Be sure they underline spelling changes and write the sentence in which they found the word on the back. Once your **er** bulletin board is started, be sure to give the children a few weeks to hunt for this suffix in their reading. This hunting step is crucial because your big goal is not just to teach the suffix but to establish the habit in your students of noticing new words in their reading and asking themselves if the new word has word parts they

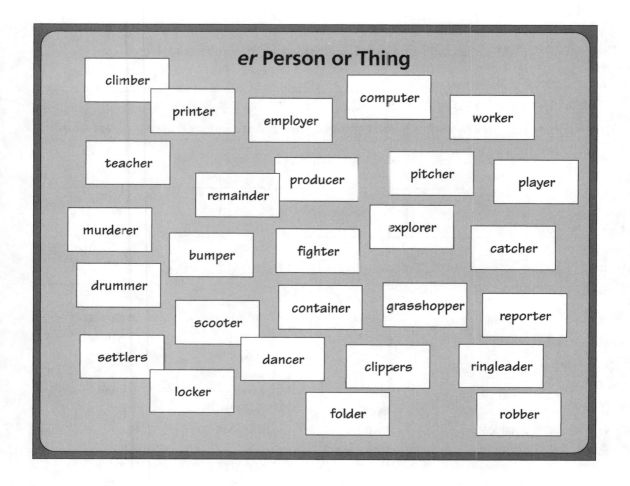

er Person or Thing

climber
printer
computer
employer
worker
teacher
producer
pitcher
player
remainder
murderer
explorer
catcher
bumper
fighter
drummer
container
grasshopper
reporter
scooter
settlers
dancer
clippers
ringleader
locker
folder
robber

know. Making the time for students to hunt words in their reading is the transfer step in word-part instruction.

When your **er** bulletin board is completed, have your students do a quick-write in which they use as many **er** words as they can. Give them a time limit and permission to make their stories silly. Remember that to truly own a word, we must use it in speaking and writing. The group work involved in identifying words in newspaper articles and categorizing words gives students a real reason to "speak" these words. Silly quick-writes provide a fun way of having students write the words.

There are three other suffixes that commonly indicate a person that does something. These are not common enough for your students to hunt, but they could be alerted to these by working in groups to categorize words. Here are some common **ian**, **or**, and **ist** words for students to categorize.

ist Person	*ist* Not a Suffix	*ian* Person	*ian* Not a Suffix	*or* Person	*or* Not a Suffix

actor	dentist	Italian	psychiatrist
alligator	director	journalist	psychologist
beautician	editor	librarian	razor
biologist	electrician	magician	resist
Californian	enlist	Martian	Russian
Canadian	exist	meteor	sailor
collector	favor	musician	scientist
colonist	flavor	odor	sculptor
color	florist	optimist	senator
comedian	governor	organist	specialist
conductor	guardian	persist	survivor
conqueror	historian	pessimist	tourist
counselor	Indian	pianist	typist
cyclist	insist	politician	visitor
custodian	inventor	professor	warrior

Teaching **ful** and **less**

Two other common suffixes that add meaning to words are **ful** and **less**. Some root words make new words with both **ful** and **less** and the words take on an opposite meaning. **Hopeful** and **hopeless** are perhaps the best example of this. Other words combine with one but not the other, as in **beautiful** and **homeless**. Most students know a lot of words that end in **ful** and **less** and understand the meanings of these suffixes, so they are relatively easy to teach. To teach these suffixes in a quick and effective way, have students work in groups to decide which roots make a word with **ful** and which with **less** and write them in the appropriate columns. Be sure students know some words can be combined with both and remind them of the **y** changing to **i** spelling change needed if the root word ends in **y**.

Words with Suffix *less* Meaning "Without"	Words with Suffix *ful* Meaning "Full" or "Having"

arm	doubt	home	penny	speech
beauty	dread	hope	pity	spoon
bottom	end	limit	play	thank
breath	fear	meaning	plenty	thought
care	forget	mercy	power	truth
cheer	fruit	mouth	price	use
cloud	harm	pain	rest	waste
color	help	peace	score	wonder

When the chart is complete, have students write sentences contrasting the words that have the same root and the opposite meaning in the same sentence. Give them an example or two to get them started:

We were **powerless** when we got hit by the **powerful** storm.

I was **hopeful** our team would win but the other team was so hot it was **hopeless**.

Teaching **able** and **ible**

The final suffixes that add meaning to words and that are relatively easy for students to understand are **able** and **ible**. Have students work in groups to sort words into four categories.

able Suffix meaning "Able"	*able* Not a Suffix	*ible* Suffix Meaning "Able"	*ible* Not a Suffix

acceptable	distractible	miserable	suitable
adjustable	dishonorable	movable	syllable
adorable	eligible	permissible	terrible
affordable	enjoyable	possible	unavoidable
agreeable	excitable	predictable	uncomfortable
available	fashionable	preferable	undesirable
believable	favorable	profitable	unfavorable
breakable	flexible	questionable	unforgettable
capable	gullible	reasonable	unstable
comfortable	horrible	recyclable	unsuitable
compatible	impossible	reliable	usable
convertible	indescribable	resistible	valuable
corruptible	inseparable	respectable	vegetable
dependable	laughable	responsible	washable
desirable	likable	reusable	workable
digestible	lovable	sensible	

Teaching **ous**, **al**, and **y**

Ous, **al**, and **y** are common suffixes that don't change the meaning of words, but rather change the word's grammatical function or part of speech. Something that is **poison** is called **poisonous**. A problem for a **nation** is a **national** problem. A day with lots of **sun** is a **sunny** day. Have students work in groups to categorize the root words according to what suffix can be added to them. The students should write the whole word—root and suffix—in the appropriate column. Remind them of spelling changes some of these words will need.

ous Words	*al* Words	*y* Words

adventure	electric	juice	poison
ambition	fame	logic	politics
bump	fog	luxury	rain
bury	fun	magic	region
caution	fury	mountain	risk
chill	globe	music	rust
cloud	glory	mystery	spine
coast	grass	nation	stick
comic	grouch	nature	sun
continue	hair	navy	thirst
curl	hazard	nerve	tribe
danger	humor	nutrition	tropics
dirt	industry	option	water
dust	joy	person	wind

Writing **ous**, **al**, **tion**, and **y** Riddles

Once the words are put into categories, have each group pick four or five words and write a riddle for the other groups to solve. Have the students write the riddle on one side of a card and the word that answers the riddle on the other side. Have them begin each riddle by telling which suffix the word ends with. Give them a few examples to get them started.

I end in **ous**. I make you laugh when I am a story. What am I?

I end in **y**. I make you want to get something to drink. What am I?

Teaching **ment**, **ance**, **ness**, and **tion**

Ment, **ance**, **ness**, and **tion** are common suffixes that don't change the meaning of words, but rather change the word's grammatical function or part of speech. We try to **equip** our army with the very best **equipment**. The money we are **allowed** to spend each week is our **allowance**. When you feel **happy**, you are experiencing **happiness**. We hold **celebrations** to **celebrate** weddings and birthdays. Have students work in groups to categorize the root words according to what suffix can be added to them. Students should write the whole word—with root and suffix—in the appropriate column. Remind them of spelling changes some of these words will need.

ment Words	*ance* Words	*ness* Words	*tion* Words

accept	advertise	annoy	assign	aware
act	agree	appear	attach	bitter
adjust	allow	argue	attend	bright
adopt	amaze	arrange	attract	clear

collect	disturb	happy	manage	rely
command	donate	ill	measure	replace
complete	educate	illustrate	migrate	require
connect	elect	impeach	move	resist
construct	employ	improve	mutate	restrict
contradict	encourage	indicate	open	rotate
contribute	endure	inflate	pave	sad
convict	engage	inject	pay	select
correct	enjoy	insure	persecute	settle
corrupt	equip	interact	place	ship
dark	excite	interrupt	predict	sick
develop	execute	intervene	prevent	state
devote	fair	introduce	produce	subtract
direct	fit	invent	promote	treat
disagree	forgive	invest	punish	weak
disappear	good	isolate	quest	
disappoint	govern	kind	ready	
distort	great	lazy	reduce	
distract	guide	locate	reject	

Writing **ment**, **ance**, **tion**, and **ness** Riddles

Once the words are put into categories, have each group pick four or five words and write a riddle for the other groups to solve. Have the students write the riddle on one side of a card and the word that answers the riddle on the other side. Have them begin each riddle by telling which suffix the word ends with. Give them a few examples to get them started.

I end in **tion**. We learned to do this in math. What am I?

I end in **ance**. You need me if you want to drive a car. What am I?

Teaching **ly**

Ly is the other suffix that occurs often enough to merit teaching to elementary children. Words that end in **ly** are often adverbs that modify verbs, adjectives, or sometimes other adverbs. Because students know a lot of **ly** words and because almost all words that end in **ly** are adverbs, you can use the procedure described earlier for **un** and **er**. Read an article to your students and have them stop you when you read a word that ends in **ly** by shouting, "Stop! *Ly!*"

Write these **ly** words on index cards and talk about how **ly** changes how a word can be used in a sentence. Put students in groups and have them brainstorm some **ly** words to begin the **ly** board. They should write the word with a marker on one side of an index card and write a sentence with that word in pencil on the other side. Attach the cards with **ly** words from what you read to them and those brainstormed by each group to begin an **ly** board. Let students hunt for **ly** words in everything they read for a week or two. Because some words that end in **ly** are not adverbs—such as **silly**, **hilly**, and **family**—provide some index cards of a different color on which students can write these words. Be sure students write the sentence in which they found the word on the back of the card. This encourages them to look for **ly** words when reading and discourages them from just writing any **ly** words they can think of.

Every day, take a few minutes to talk about the meanings of the newly added **ly** words. Because these words often show action, they lend themselves nicely to pantomime games. Let volunteers choose a word from the board and "mime" that word. The person who correctly guesses the word can mime the next word if he or she chooses.

Accelerating Vocabulary Growth for English Language Learners

Word parts are especially difficult for children who are not native English speakers, but because English is such a morphologically complex language, they do need to learn the most common prefixes and suffixes and how these change the meaning and grammatical function of words when added to root words. If you have a student whose native language is Spanish or French, cognates—words that have the same root or origin—can help him or her learn English words by looking for familiar parts. The cognate chart lists French and Spanish cognates for common English words.

Spanish and French Cognates for Common English Words

English	Spanish	French
accent	acento	accent
accident	accidente	accident
active	activo	actif
actor	actor	acteur
admire, admiration	admirar, admiración	admirer, admiration
admission	admisión	admission
adore	adorar	adorer
adult	adulto	adulte
agriculture	agricultura	agriculture
alphabet	alfabeto	alphabet
ambition, ambitious	ambición, ambicioso	ambition, ambitieux
animal	animal	animal
apartment	apartamento	appartement
April	abril	avril
arrange	n/a	arranger
arrive	n/a	arriver
artist	artista	artiste
attraction	atracción	attraction
bank	banco	banque
bicycle	bicicleta	bicyclette
biography	biografía	biographie
block	bloque	bloc
blue	n/a	bleu
calendar	calendario	calendrier
calm	calma	calme
cancel	cancelar	n/a
capital (n)	capital	capitale
captain (n)	capitán	capitaine
carpenter	carpintero	n/a

(continued)

English	Spanish	French
category	categoría	catégorie
center, central	centro, central	centre, central
change (n)	n/a	changement
character (attributes of an individual)	carácter	caractére
chocolate	chocolate	chocolat
color	color	couleur
comfortable	confortable	confortable
comic (adj)	cómico	comique
commercial (adj)	comercial	commercial
confidence	confianza	confiance
conflict	conflicto	conflict
construction	construcción	construction
continue	continuar	continuer
cousin	n/a	cousin
credit	crédito	crédit
culture	cultura	culture
dance	n/a	danser
December	diciembre	décembre
decision	decisión	décision
defend	defender	défendre
democracy	democracia	démocratie
dentist	dentista	dentiste
department	departamento	département
desert (n)	desierto	désert
destruction	destrucción	destruction
detail (n)	detalle	détail
determine	determinar	déterminer
dictionary	diccionario	dictionnaire
dinner	n/a	dîner

English	Spanish	French
direction/director	dirección/director	direction/directeur
economy	economía	économie
education	educación	éducation
elementary	elemental	élémentaire
energy	energía	énergie
error	error	erreur
excellent	excelente	excellent
except (conj)	excepto	excepté
exercise (n)	ejercicio	exercice
extreme	extremo	extrême
fault (n)	falta	faute
finish (v)	n/a	finir
friction	fricción	friction
fruit	fruta	fruit
function	función	fonction
gallon	galón	gallon
gas (not gasoline)	gas	gaz
general (adj)	general	général
government	gobierno	gouvernement
habit	hábito	habitude
history	historia	histoire
honor (n)	honor	honneur
hospital	hospital	hôpital
hotel	hotel	hôtel
human	humano	humain
idea	idea	idée
illegal	ilegal	illégal
imagine	imaginar	imaginer
impressive	impresionante	impressionnant
individual (n)	individuo	individu

(continued)

English	Spanish	French
insect	insecto	insecte
insist (v)	insistir	insister
invent	inventar	inventer
invite	invitar	inviter
jacket	n/a	jaquette
labor	labor	labour
lamp	lámpara	lampe
legal	legal	légal
letter (of alphabet)	letra	lettre
liberty	libertad	liberté
magnificent	magnífico	magnifique
mark	marca	marque
message	mensaje	message
minute	minuto	minute
motor	motor	moteur
music	música	musique
national	nacional	national
notice (v)	notar	noter
November	noviembre	novembre
number	número	nombre
object (v)	objetar	objecter
observe	observar	observer
opinion	opinión	opinion
palace	palacio	palais
parade	parada	parade
part (n)	parte	part, or partie
pass (v)	pasar	passer
pharmacy	farmacia	pharmacie
planet	planeta	planète
plate	plato	n/a

English	Spanish	French
poet	poeta	poète
politics	política	politique
practice (n)	práctica	pratique
prefer	preferir	préférer
prepare	preparar	préparer
president	presidente	présicent
pretend	pretender	prétendre
prevention	prevención	prévention
principal (adj)	principal	principal
process	proceso	procés
producer, product	productor, producto	producteur, produit
program (n)	programa	programme
protest (v)	protestar	protester
radio	radio	radio
respond	responder	répondre
restaurant	restaurante	restaurant
result	resultado	résultat
salad	ensalada	salade
science	ciencia	science
September	septiembre	septembre
solid	sólido	solide
soup	sopa	soupe
special	especial	spécial
table	n/a	table
telephone	teléfono	téléphone
television	televisión	télévision
urban	urbano	urbain
vacant, vacation	vacante, vacación	vacant, vacances
visit (n)	visita	visite

✿ Roots

This chapter began by suggesting that you begin your word-part instruction with compound words. Compound words have two root words. Once your students begin to understand how prefixes and suffixes help them connect meanings to words, they enjoy working with roots to see how many words they can construct. Of course, you will want to start with the most common and predictable root or base words. The word *play* occurs in such related words as *replay*, *playground*, and *playoffs*. *Work* is part of many words, including *workers*, *workout*, and *workstation*. *Place* is another common base word and students often know the meaning of *placemats*, *replace*, and *workplace*. *Light* occurs in many words, including *lightning*, *headlights*, and *enlighten*. *Form* is the root for almost 100 words, including *formation*, *deformity*, and *platform*. *Time* can be found in numerous words, including *timeout*, *overtime*, and *timekeeper*. *Fire* occurs in words such as *misfire*, *fireplace*, and *fireworks*. *Ball* is part of many compound words, including *meatball*, *eyeball*, and *ballpark*. Students enjoy building

Word Tree

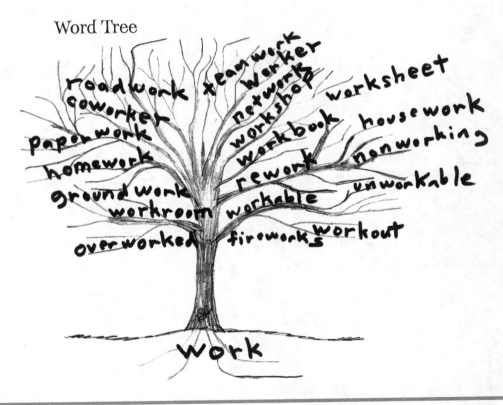

word trees. The root word is the root of the tree and the branches are all the words that share that root. Once students have constructed a tree, challenge them to write a paragraph using as many of the words on the tree as they can.

There is disagreement among vocabulary experts in terms of teaching students Latin and Greek roots. It is true that these roots do contain clues to meaning, but the meaning relationships are often hard to figure out and students might get discouraged if they cannot "ferret out" the meaning of a word based on the meaning of the root. Perhaps the most sensible way for elementary teachers to approach Greek and Latin roots is to be aware of them and to point out relationships when they think these will be understandable to most

Root	Meaning	Common Examples
dict	say	dictator, contradict, dictionary, unpredictable, verdict
duct	lead	duct, conductor, reduce, deduction, abduct, educate
fac/fec	do, make	factory, manufacture, benefactor, effect, defect
ject	throw	inject, reject, interject, object, subject, eject
loc	place	locate, location, relocate, dislocate, local
meter	measure	metric, kilometer, barometer, thermometer, diameter
micro	small	microphone, microscope, micromanage, microcosm
phon	sound	telephone, phonics, symphony, microphone, phonograph
photo	light	photograph, photography, telephoto, photosynthesis
port	carry, take	report, heliport, transportation, export, import, portable
press	press	impress, depression, pressure, express, oppression, compress
scrib	write	scribble, describe, prescription, subscribe, transcript
sens	feel	sense, sensitive, insensitive, sensation, consent, nonsense
spec	look	inspector, spectacle, respect, spectator, suspect, prospect
struct	build	structure, construct, reconstruction, instructor, destruction
tele	far	television, telegraph, telepathy, telephoto, telecommunication
tract	drag, pull	tractor, extract, contract, contraction, attract, subtraction
vis/vid	see	vision, revise, invisible, video, evidence
voc	voice, call	vocal, vocalize, advocate, vocation, convocation, provoke

children. When encountering the word *spectacle*, for example, you might explain that a spectacle is something a person sees that is quite striking or unusual. Furthermore, you might point out that the root *spect* means "to watch" and invite the students to think about how words they know, such as *inspection* and *spectators*, are related to this meaning. The word *constructive* could be explained as "helpful" or "building up" as opposed to *destructive*, which is "unhelpful" or "tearing down." Students might be told that the root *struct* means "to build" and asked to think about how other words they know, such as *structure* and *reconstruction*, are related to this meaning. The Greek and Latin roots chart on page 67 lists roots that have high utility in words elementary students read. When a word containing one of these roots occurs, it may be worth exploring the root meaning with your students.

✤ The Magic of Morphemes

Morphemes—prefixes, suffixes, and roots—are the building blocks of English words. Morphemes are magical because when your students know how to do the tricks, they can turn one word into six or seven. Use the hunting and sorting activities in this chapter to turn all your students into morpheme magicians!

chapter 4

Maximizing Vocabulary Growth During Reading Lessons

Stop ten elementary teachers and ask them when they teach vocabulary, and nine out of ten will quickly respond, "Before children read."

Introducing new vocabulary before children read is so engrained in the minds of most elementary teachers that its utility and effectiveness are never even questioned. Let's begin thinking about the proper role of vocabulary instruction during reading lessons by considering how effective traditional before-reading vocabulary introduction is.

In a typical reading lesson, the teacher selects eight to ten words that students might not know and introduces these words by writing them on the board, asking someone to tell what each word means and asking someone else to use the word in a sentence. The students then read the selection containing these words and, hopefully, notice and connect meanings for the words introduced. In some classrooms, children then follow up the reading by looking up the vocabulary words and copying definitions. If there will be a test on these vocabulary words, students memorize the definitions they copied.

The questions we must ask ourselves are: "How effective is this traditional reading vocabulary instruction?" and "How many children who didn't already have these words in their meaning vocabularies will add these words based on these traditional activities?" If we are honest with ourselves, most of us know the answers: Traditional vocabulary instruction in which words are introduced, words are encountered in one text, and definitions are copied and memorized does little to move students toward acquiring those 1,000 to 3,000 new words they need to learn each year. Sometimes, tradition is a good thing. In the case of vocabulary instruction as part of reading lessons, tradition results in thousands of teachers wasting valuable time and energy in a daily routine that accomplishes little.

This chapter will suggest some radical changes in the way you approach vocabulary instruction during reading. As you read the chapter, think about this big question: "How can vocabulary instruction during reading be done in a way that will result in children who did not already know the meanings for the words adding many of the words to their meaning vocabulary stores?"

Choose Vocabulary Words as if You Were Paying for Each Word and Needed to Keep Them Forever

When we shop for staples—shoes, for example—there are many, many choices. We know what we need and we know that we can't afford all the shoes in the store. Perhaps we find a cute pair of black shoes and then we remember how many pairs of cute black shoes we already have in our closets. We find some green shoes we like and there are no green shoes in our closets, but then we wonder where we would wear the green shoes and what we would wear them with. We find some cute strappy sandals, but then we imagine walking on the four-inch heels! We find a pair of very comfortable slip-on shoes but, on second look, they are really ugly! Finally, we settle on the perfect (we hope!) pair of shoes—stylish but comfortable, different from our other shoes, but not too different—and a perfect fit.

The first step in increasing the effectiveness of your vocabulary instruction is to be very picky about the words you choose to teach. The biggest mistake teachers make in picking words is to select words solely because the words are unknown to their students. Sometimes we even feel compelled to introduce a word because we don't know what that word means and if we don't know it, surely our students won't know it! Words whose meanings you have to look up are not apt to be words worth spending your vocabulary allowance on. Remember the concept of "Goldilocks words" from Chapter 2. Isabel Beck and colleagues (2002) refer to these words as "Tier 2" words: words many students don't know but that will be useful to them—not too common, not too obscure—just-right words. These are the words that your students are most apt to add to their vocabulary stores.

Once you have a list of possible Goldilocks words, think about the selection your students are going to read. How important is each word to comprehending the selection? If a word is a Goldilocks word but appears only once in the selection and is not essential to comprehending the selection, that word is probably like the green shoes—nice but not essential for this reading lesson.

Another factor to consider is whether the word has a word part you would like students to focus on. Does the word have a root, prefix, or suffix you have taught and that will remind students of the usefulness of asking the word-part question: "Does that new word have any word parts I know?" You might choose a Goldilocks word that is not crucial to comprehending the selection if that word will allow you to refocus your students' attention on a common word part.

To maximize the effectiveness of vocabulary instruction during reading lessons, select each word by asking these questions:

- Is this word one most of my students don't have a rich meaning for?

- Is this a word my students need to know and could use in speaking and writing?

- Is this word essential to understanding the selection my students will be reading?

- Does this word have a word part I want to focus on?

When you choose your words based on these criteria, you know you have words worth the time and energy it will take to teach them.

In selecting the perfect words, try to include one or two words students should be able to figure out for themselves based on the context, pictures, and word parts. In Chapter 2, it was suggested that you maximize the number of words your students could learn from their independent reading by modeling how to figure out meanings using the Three Read-Aloud Words strategy. After students begin to understand how this works, it was suggested that one day each week be designated a sticky-note day and that students should be given one sticky note that they should attach to a word they figured out during their independent reading.

This strategy can easily be extended to reading lessons. Include in the words you will teach for each selection one word that meets your criteria—not known by your students but needs to be known, important to the selection or containing a word part you want to focus on, can be figured out by most students based on context, pictures, or word parts. After introducing (in whatever way you choose) the other words, give students one sticky note and have them pronounce and write the "mystery word" on it. Just as you did for independent reading, resist the urge to provide the meaning for the word or let anyone tell a meaning for it. Tell students that you want them to be detectives for this word. Their first job as detectives will be to locate the word in the text. When they locate the word, they should place the sticky note on the sentence containing the word and look for clues to solve the mystery of what that word means. Ask students what clues they might find and have them verbalize that to figure out what a word means in a reading selection, they can use context—the words and sentences around the word, pictures, and word parts.

⚒ Introducing Words Before Students Read

When introducing vocabulary, you should implement the principles for effective vocabulary development outlined in Chapter 1:

- Students develop meanings for words through multiple and varied encounters with those words.
- Vocabulary is learned best when it is based on real, concrete experiences.
- Pictures and other visuals help solidify word meanings.
- To truly own a word, children must use that word in speaking and writing.

Look at the words you are planning to teach and think about these principles. Could any of the words be introduced using real or concrete experiences? Are there any pictures in the selection or readily available on the Internet that would make the concept clear? How could you quickly get students to make an initial connection with these words through speaking and writing? The way you introduce vocabulary words is going to vary depending on your resources and the particular words, but consider these possibilities.

Real, Concrete, Hands-On Experiences

Providing real, concrete, hands-on experiences is often not possible during a reading lesson because of resource and time limitations. The feasibility of these real, concrete, hands-on experiences during math, science, art, music, and physical education is one of the major reasons for directly teaching a large number of the needed 1,000 to 3,000 new words while teaching these subject areas. But sometimes you can quickly provide something real or concrete, and asking yourself if this is feasible each time you think about how to teach vocabulary increases the chances that it can happen.

Are there any objects in your classroom that are examples of the concept you are trying to introduce? What if the word you want to teach is **equipment**? Could you get together some things used to perform a certain task and explain that all these separate things together are your writing **equipment** or your painting **equipment**? If you wanted to introduce the word **flexible**, could you point to some objects in the room that are **flexible** and some that are not? What if the word were **essential**? What objects in your classroom are **essential** to learning?

Besides the physical objects in your room, you have another ready resource for providing quick and easy real experiences with new vocabulary words. You! Could you do anything to act out any of the words? Imagine, for example, that one of your chosen words is **accidental**. Could you act out a scene in which you broke something and then had to explain to the owner that you didn't do it on purpose? It was **accidental**. What if the word were **envious**? Could you pretend that a teacher friend had won a marvelous vacation and then talk about how **envious** you are? What if the word were **pedestrian**? Could you act out crossing a street and declare your outrage when a car almost hits you and explain that **pedestrians** have the right of way at all crosswalks? Students love it when their teachers "ham it up," and most elementary teachers are natural actors. Not every vocabulary word lends itself to dramatization, but some do and when you find yourself thinking about introducing a word that you could model, take the stage and have some fun!

Before moving on to thinking about how to provide visual experience with new words, consider the six words for which you could easily provide real experience.

equipment   flexible   essential   accidental   envious   pedestrians

All these words have word parts you may want your students to think about. After showing them some equipment in your room, write the word **equipment** and ask your students if this word contains any parts they know. Then help them see the **equip-equipment** relationship by using both words in a sentence such as:

> To do anything, we need to **equip** ourselves with the necessary tools, which we call **equipment**.

You can do the same thing with **flex-flexible**, **accident-accidental**, and **envy-envious**.

> When we can **flex** or bend something, we say that thing is **flexible**.
> When something happens by **accident**, we say it was **accidental**.
> When you **envy** something, we say you are **envious**.

Essential and **pedestrian** also have word parts—but they are less obvious and you may not want to point them out if your students are not ready to see the links. Most students who are not familiar with the word **essential** also don't know the word **essence**. **Ped** is the Latin root for foot and you might help children to connect this word to something they know by using the familiar words **pedal** and **pedicure**. **Pedestrian** ends in **ian** as do many other words that name types of people, including **librarian**, **magician**, and **veterinarian**.

It is not always possible to provide real experience with words students will meet in their reading but sometimes it is. Not all words have word parts you can point out to students to help them connect meanings, but many do. If every time you introduce vocabulary words before reading you utilize whatever real experience and word parts are possible, you maximize the possibility that your students will actually add these new words to their store of vocabulary words.

Virtual Reality

New vocabulary generally falls into two categories. Many of the new words students meet are new words for known concepts, such as **equipment**, **flexible**, **essential**, **accidental**, **envious**, and **pedestrians**. Perhaps most of your students have the concepts—just not the words.

equipment—stuff you need for particular tasks
flexible—bendable
essential—you have to have it
accidental—not done on purpose
envious—wishing you had something someone else had
pedestrian—person walking on a street

New words for known concepts are much easier to teach than new words for new concepts. For my first-graders in northern Florida, **escalator**, **park**, and **restaurant** were new words for new concepts. Not only did they not know the words, they had never experienced the things represented by the words. Children in Hawaii know all about oceans but deserts and canyons are probably new concepts for Hawaiian children. Native American children living on reservations in Arizona certainly have the concepts for **deserts** and **canyons**, but probably not for **oceans** and **volcanoes**. Of course, providing concrete experiences for new words/new concepts is the best vocabulary introduction, but often this is impossible. When you can't provide real experiences, ask yourself if there is any way to provide virtual experiences. One of the very best uses for Web technology is your ability to take your students on virtual field-trips. In some classrooms, equipped with SMART Boards and wired for the Internet, this virtual experience can be a part of each day's plan for vocabulary development. In other schools, you may have to plan to provide virtual experiences when you and your students can be scheduled into the media center or computer lab. Regardless of how accessible technology is in your classroom, your vocabulary introduction will be richer and more engaging if you make use of whatever virtual fieldtrips are possible.

Pictures and Other Visual Representations

In addition to virtual fieldtrips, the Web provides every teacher with an endless source of visuals, including pictures, photos, and other graphic representations. Instead of bulky file folders full of pictures, savvy teachers today compile files of images stored on one slim disc. Because these images are so available and easily stored, you don't have to settle for just one picture but can have a dozen or more images to represent a concept. Search for "canyon" images and you will find pictures of both the Grand Canyon and a small unnamed canyon in the Himalayas. Having a variety of images for a new word that is also a new concept allows you to provide a richer introduction to that word and allows your students to broaden their concept from the start.

In addition to the wide range of visual images available on the Web, there is a source of readily available pictures often ignored when teachers think about introducing vocabulary. The text your students are going to read often contains illustrations that clarify the meanings of new words. Marie Clay (1991) developed the idea of a Picture Walk to introduce new vocabulary. This activity is most often used with young children but has enormous potential for vocabulary development with older students and with English language learners.

Picture Walks

After you have decided on the words you want to introduce to students before they read, look at the pictures in the selection and see if you can use any of them to build the vocabulary. Nouns represented by the pictures will be the most obvious possibilities but pictures can also help you build meaning for verbs and adjectives. Imagine, for example, that the selection you are going to have students read is about volcanoes. The title page shows the volcano erupting and the people fleeing the village. Four of your chosen vocabulary words—**volcano**, **eruption**, **evacuating**, and **terrified**—could be introduced using this one picture. Here is a script for the vocabulary introduction you might use for these four words:

> "Boys and girls, let's look at the picture on the title page of our story and think about some vocabulary words that go with the picture."
>
> (Teacher points to volcano in picture.)

"Does anyone know what we call this?"

(One student responds that it is a volcano.)

"Yes, that is called a volcano. A volcano is a . . . ."

(Teacher shows an index card with the word **volcano** written on it and has everyone say the word **volcano**.)

"Show me a thumbs up if you have heard the word **volcano** before."

(Most students show a thumbs up.)

"Who can tell me anything you know about volcanoes?"

(Students share experiences with volcanoes and teacher helps them access whatever knowledge they have by asking questions.)

"Has anyone ever seen a real volcano?"

"Have you ever seen a volcano in a picture or movie?"

"Are there any volcanoes in our state?"

"Where could you go to see a volcano?"

(Teacher points to fire and debris coming out of volcano.)

"What is happening with this volcano?"

"What is coming out of the top?"

"Does the volcano always look like this, with lava and steam spouting out?"

"Does anyone know the word we use to describe a volcano what has lava and steam spouting out of it?"

(No one volunteers the word so teacher shows students the word **eruption** written on an index card.)

"When fire and debris spout out of the top of the volcano like this, we call that an eruption. Everyone say **eruption**."

(Students chorally pronounce **eruption**. Teacher supplies a "kid-friendly" definition of **eruption**.)

"Do you recognize any familiar word parts in the word **eruption**?"

(Students say that they know the **tion** part. Teacher writes the word **erupt** under **eruption** and uses the two words in a sentence.)

"This volcano is erupting. When a volcano erupts, we call that an **eruption**. **Erupt** and **eruption** are related words, just like **collect** and **collection**. If we collect baseball cards, you call this your baseball card . . . ."

(Teacher pauses and students quickly supply the word **collection**. Teacher gives a few more examples of **tion** words students know.)

"When you connect two things, we call this a . . . ."

"When someone interrupts us, we call this an . . . ."

(Teacher has students pronounce **eruption** one more time and asks them what **eruption** means. Students respond that **eruption** is what you call it when the lava and steam come out of the volcano. Teacher then directs their attention to the people in the picture.)

"Now look at the people. What are they doing?"

(Students respond that they are leaving, running away because the fire is dangerous. Teacher shows the index card with the word **evacuating**.)

"When people leave a place quickly because it is dangerous, we say they are evacuating. Everyone say **evacuating**."

(Students chorally pronounce **evacuating**.)

"We don't have to evacuate our town because of volcanoes, but sometimes we do have to evacuate because of something else that is very dangerous."

(Students immediately think of hurricanes and how they have had to evacuate their homes along the coast and go inland when a strong hurricane was coming. They eagerly share their experiences with hurricanes, and the teacher encourages them to use the new word **evacuated** to describe the very well known concept of leaving their homes when a hurricane approaches.)

"There is one more word we can use this picture to help us build meaning for. Look at the faces of the people who are evacuating because the volcano is erupting. Show me with your faces what their faces look like."

(Students eagerly mimic frightened expressions and explain that the people look like this because they are worried and scared and frightened.)

> "Exactly. They are worried and scared and very frightened. Here is a word that means not just a little scared and frightened but very, very scared and frightened."

(Teacher shows the word **terrified** and students pronounce it.)

> "Were you terrified when you had to evacuate because the hurricane was coming? Have you ever been so scared or frightened by anything else that if someone looked at your face he or she would say you were terrified?"

(Students eagerly share experiences of being really frightened. Teacher responds by using the word **terrified** to describe their feelings.)

> "I bet you were terrified when you watched that scary movie all by yourself."

> "I would be terrified too if I were camping and I saw a bear outside my tent."

In this Picture Walk example, the picture on the title page of the book provided visual support for the introduction of four vocabulary words. Many times, you may want to use several different pictures on different pages to introduce vocabulary. Imagine that your students are about to read an informational selection about animals. You have chosen several animal names to introduce to your students along with the word **habitat**. Your Picture Walk introduction might sound like this:

> "Boys and girls, look at the animal on this page. Do you know what this animal is called?"

(If a student names the animal, teacher agrees. If not, teacher continues.)

> "This animal is called a buffalo."

(Teacher shows the word **buffalo** and has the students pronounce it. To get them to use the word **buffalo**, you ask them to compare a buffalo to another animal they know. Teacher continues.)

"In what ways does the buffalo look like other animals?"

(Students respond.)

"The buffalo has horns like a deer."

"The buffalo has hair like a horse."

"The buffalo has hooves like a cow."

"Very good. Now look at the animal on this page. Can anyone name this animal?"

You continue drawing students' attention to all the animals whose names you have chosen to introduce. For each one, you turn to the page with the picture of the animal and ask if anyone knows the name. If someone knows the name, you acknowledge that and show the index card with the animal name on it and have everyone pronounce the name. You then provide students an opportunity to explore the attributes of this animal and use the animal name by asking them to compare the animal to other animals they know. After comparing each animal, tell students that they will learn lots more about the animal when they read about it and that information will be shared after reading. It is not necessary to introduce all the animal names in the book—only the ones you think many of your students don't know.

To introduce the word **habitat**, draw students' attention to several pictures in the book that show where each animal lives. Show them the word **habitat** on an index card and tell them that an animal's habitat is where that animal lives. Let students describe the habitat for the pictures you are looking at by starting each sentence with the animal's name and the word **habitat**:

"The buffalo's habitat is the . . . ."

"The giraffe's habitat is the . . . ."

"The peacock's habitat is the . . . ."

When you do a Picture Walk with students, you make use of the pictures in the selection to connect new words to old concepts and to build new concepts. For many of the students about to read the story about the volcano, the words **volcano** and **eruption** were new words for new concepts. Most students had experienced evacuating and feeling terrified. For them, the words

terrified and **evacuated** were new words for known concepts. For students who have no experience with the animal names you introduced, these words would be new words for new concepts. Because most students have the concept of "the place where you live," the word **habitat** is probably a new word for a known concept.

The "Goldilocks" vocabulary you choose to introduce to your students is always apt to be a combination of new words for new concepts and new words for old concepts. Because your students have had different experiences, lived in different places, watched different videos, and read different books, words that are new words for new concepts for some of your students will simply be new words for old concepts for other students. Regardless of which type of word you are introducing, pictures along with real and virtual experience provide a rich and engaging introduction to new words.

Context Clues

If you are doing the Three Read-Aloud Words activity regularly and having students share how they figured out the meaning of a sticky-note word in their own reading one day each week, you are teaching students to use context to figure out the meanings of unfamiliar words. If you are regularly taking your students on Picture Walks before reading, you are teaching them how new words are often brought to life by the pictures in the text. This regular attention to how context and pictures make word meanings clear is probably the best instruction you can do so that your students get in the habit of and know how to use pictures and context. One caution you may need to point out to students is that context does not always directly reveal the meanings of unfamiliar words and can sometimes be misleading. Imagine that the only reference in the text to the word **incredulously** is in this sentence:

"Her dad listened incredulously."

This context does not provide much of a clue to the meaning of this new word.

On the other hand, the text might continue with much richer context:

> "Her dad listened incredulously. 'I find what you are telling me really hard to believe,' he admitted when she had finished explaining how the accident had happened."

How much context helps with meaning varies greatly. If a word is important and context is slim, students need to use the dictionary to figure out a meaning that might make sense in the context of what they are reading.

Here is another example of how context can sometimes be misleading. One student put a sticky note on the word **grimaced** and explained that the word meant "yelled." The sentence in which the student had read the word was:

> "The waiter in the crowded restaurant grimaced as the tray slid to the floor."

The teacher explained to the student that "yelled" would make sense there but that the waiter could have done many things and there really wasn't enough context to decide exactly what the waiter did. The child quickly looked up the word **grimaced** in the dictionary and the teacher led the whole class to twist their faces into the grimace they might make if they had just dropped a whole tray of food in a crowded restaurant.

As children are sharing their sticky-note words, you will have many opportunities to show them both how the context can be extremely helpful and how it can lead them astray. You can also model how a dictionary is best used—to clarify meaning and to let the reader know if the meaning he or she inferred from context is indeed the right one.

Kid-Friendly Definitions

Real, virtual, or picture experience is always required when introducing new words that are also new concepts for your students. When the words you want to introduce to students are new words for concepts they already know, you can introduce vocabulary to students by providing them with "kid-friendly" definitions. In Chapter 3 of a splendid book on teaching vocabulary,

Bringing Words to Life (Beck, McKeown & Kucan, 2002), the authors contrast dictionary definitions with what they call "student-friendly explanations." They cite dictionary definitions such as "one associated with another," "appearance or feeling that misleads because it is not real," and "break up; split" and ask the reader how helpful these definitions would be if they did not already know the meanings for the target words: **ally**, **allusion**, and **disrupt** (pp. 36–37).

The authors explain that dictionary definitions are often very unhelpful because space limitations require them to be concise and general. Because dictionary definitions are so brief and unspecific, students who don't already know the meanings of the words are often misled. If **disrupt** means "break up" or "split," your students might think they could disrupt a candy bar to share with a friend! If **erode** means "eat out," this sentence written by a student to use **erode** in a sentence makes perfect sense!

My family likes to erode on weekends.

Rather than present students with dictionary definitions, Beck, McKeown, and Kucan suggest giving students student-friendly explanations that characterize the word and explain meanings in everyday language. For **ally**, instead of the vague dictionary definition, "one associated with another," their student-friendly explanation is:

"someone who helps you in what you are trying to do, especially when there are other people against you." (p. 36)

For **allusion**, instead of "appearance or feeling that misleads because it is not real," the authors suggest:

"something that looks like one thing but is really something else or is not there at all." (p. 37)

For **disrupt**, instead of "break up; split," their student-friendly explanation is:

"to cause difficulties that stop something from continuing easily or peacefully." (p. 37)

Student-friendly explanations are one way to introduce your students to words for which they already have a concept and only need to connect the new word to the old concept. With any type of vocabulary introduction, it is crucial that students have a chance to use the word for which you have provided an explanation. The easiest way to assure your students are actively involved in your vocabulary introduction is to seat them in "talking partners" and have them "turn and talk." After providing your student-friendly explanations for **ally, allusion**, and **disrupt**, for example, have the students connect their experiences to these words by giving them a "turn and talk" task.

> "Turn and talk to your partner about an ally you have had—someone who helped you in something you were trying to do even if other people were against you."

> "Turn and talk to your partner about an allusion you have seen—something you saw and you thought it was one thing but it turned out to be something else or something you thought you saw but it really wasn't there."

> "Turn and talk to your partner about something that happened that disrupted an activity you were engaged in. Did the rain ever disrupt your ball game? Did a family emergency ever disrupt your vacation plans?"

To develop deep knowledge of a word, it is often helpful to think of what a word is not. After introducing the word **ally**, you could have your students turn and talk and start their sentence with:

> "A person is not an ally when . . . ."

After all your vocabulary words are introduced, you can have students do some "turn and talk" tasks that get your students to think about all the words introduced. Ask the talking partners to choose two of the vocabulary words that go together in some way. Give them a minute to do this and then ask the children which two words they chose and see if anyone can guess how these words go together. Children also enjoying making up sentences with the word and telling the class their sentence, leaving a blank for the word. Give the talking partners one minute to compose one sentence and then let them share the sentences with the class and see who can guess the vocabulary word they left out.

Carol was my _____ when she helped me clean my room.

We thought we saw a monster in the window but it was an _____.

It rained a little at the ballpark but not enough to _____ the game.

Many vocabulary words are new words for known concepts. When you are introducing vocabulary that most of your students already have concepts for, you can give them kid-friendly definitions for those words and then provide an opportunity for them to connect that word to their experience by giving them a quick turn and talk task.

Accelerating Vocabulary Growth for English Language Learners

Using real and virtual experiences and visuals to introduce vocabulary is important for all children but it is critical for children who are learning English. The majority of the words English language learners need to learn are new English words for those concepts they already know in their language. Using real and virtual experiences and pictures allows your students who are learnng English to connect what they know because they can see the concept being taught. Whenever possible, ask your English language learners to tell you the word in their language. Unfortunately, even kid-friendly definitions are not apt to be very informative for children learning English because although they may have the concept, they may not know many of the words you use in your explanation. If you have English language learners in your classroom, redouble your efforts to find or create a real, virtual, or visual introduction to new meaning vocabulary.

Rivet

Rivet is an activity I created one day while sitting in the back of a classroom watching a student teacher try to introduce some vocabulary words to her students. The vocabulary the student teacher was introducing was important to the story and the words were words most of the students had concepts for and only needed to learn the words. The student teacher was diligently writing the words on the board, giving students kid-friendly definitions and having students access meanings for the words and relate them to each other. Unfortunately, the students were not particularly interested in the words, and their attention was marginal at best. After the words had been introduced and the students began to read the selection, many of the struggling readers couldn't decode them, much less associate meaning with them. Rivet was conceived that day and has since saved many a student teacher from the dreaded experience of having taught some words that no one seemed to have learned!

When using Rivet to introduce vocabulary, select the words as you always do. Choose words that many of your students don't know but need to know as well as words that are important to the selection. Also include the names of important characters, especially if these names will be difficult for your struggling readers to decode. Sometimes, as in this lesson, you may want to include a two-word phrase if it is very important to understanding the selection. The following Rivet activity was based on the book *Arturo's Baton* by Syd Hoff.

Begin the activity by writing numbers and drawing lines on the board to indicate how many letters each word has. The board at the beginning of this rivet activity would look like this:

1. _ _ _ _ _ _ _ _ _ _
2. _ _ _ _ _ _ _ _ _ _
3. _ _ _ _ _ _ _ _ _ _
4. _ _ _ _ _ _
5. _ _ _ _ _
6. _ _ _ _ _ _ _ _ _ _
7. _ _ _ _ _ _ _ _
8. _ _ _ _ _ _

For each word, fill in the letters in order one at a time. Tell the students that they are allowed to "shout out" in a Rivet activity and that they should shout the word as soon as they think they know it. Pause briefly after you write each letter to see if anyone can guess the word. Students are not guessing letters but are trying to guess each word as soon as they think they know what it is. Most students will not be able to guess the word when the board looks like the first example. But after a few more letters are added, as in the second example, many will have some good guesses.

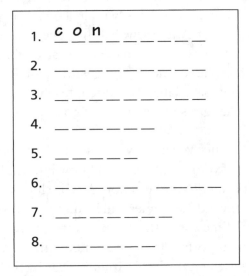

Once someone has guessed the correct word, finish writing the word, have everyone pronounce **conductor**, and ask if anyone knows what the word **conductor** means. For **conductor**, students may say that a train has a conductor. Accept the answer and ask if anything besides a train has a conductor. If students suggest orchestra or band, acknowledge those answers and then ask if they know any other meanings for the word **conductor**. If you are studying electricity in science, someone may think of that meaning of conductor. As you introduce each word, ask questions to elicit the total knowledge of the class about each word but don't give away how the word is used in the story.

After eliciting all the associations anyone in the class has with **conductor**, begin writing the letters of the second word, pausing for just a second after writing each letter to see if anyone can guess the word. The attention of all the students is generally riveted (thus the name Rivet) to each added letter, and with a few more letters many students will guess the word.

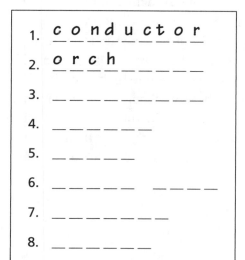

1. c o n d u c t o r
2. o r c h _ _ _ _ _
3. _ _ _ _ _ _ _ _ _
4. _ _ _ _ _ _
5. _ _ _ _ _ _
6. _ _ _ _ _ _ _ _ _ _
7. _ _ _ _ _ _ _
8. _ _ _ _ _ _

1. c o n d u c t o r
2. o r c h e s t r a
3. _ _ _ _ _ _ _ _ _
4. _ _ _ _ _ _
5. _ _ _ _ _ _
6. _ _ _ _ _ _ _ _ _ _
7. _ _ _ _ _ _ _
8. _ _ _ _ _ _

Once the word **orchestra** is completed and pronounced, ask students what they know about an orchestra. Is it different from a band? Have they ever seen an orchestra? Do they know anyone who plays in an orchestra? Now that you have the word **orchestra**, ask students how they think **conductor** and **orchestra** go together. Help students to see that in this story the meaning of conductor is probably going to be the person who "conducts" the orchestra.

Continue in this fashion until all the words have been completely written and correctly guessed. Here is what the board will look like when all words are introduced.

1. c o n d u c t o r
2. o r c h e s t r a
3. T o s c a n i n i
4. A r t u r o
5. b a t o n
6. w o r l d t o u r
7. p a j a m a s
8. c a n c e l

After writing each word and having the word pronounced, ask questions to elicit all the possible meanings of the words and any relationships students see between words. In this lesson, one student commented, "What do pajamas have to do with anything?" The teacher responded, "That is a strange word here but it turns out it is an important word in the story."

Next, you want students to use the words. To get students to process words and to use them in speech, ask them to make a prediction about something they think will happen in the story. Their prediction must use at least two of the vocabulary words. Have partners turn and talk to create their prediction together and then encourage them to share their predictions with the class. Write five or six of their predictions on the board, underlining the vocabulary words introduced.

The orchestra went on a world tour.

The conductor was Toscanini.

Arturo Toscanini was the conductor of the orchestra.

They had to cancel the concert because the orchestra wore their pajamas.

Toscanini forgot his pajamas when he took the orchestra on a world tour.

If the children fail to use some of the words in their predictions, prompt them to think about how those words might fit into the story. After asking them how the baton fits into the story, you might get these predictions:

Toscanini needed the baton to conduct the orchestra.

Toscanini got mad and threw the baton at the orchestra so they had to cancel the show.

Children generally enjoy trying to combine the important words and make predictions—some serious and some silly. The important thing is not how serious the predictions are or whether or not the predictions are right. What matters is that students are using the key vocabulary and anticipating how these words might come together to make a story.

When you have some predictions (six to eight is plenty), have the students read the selection to see if any of the predictions were true. After the students have read the selection, ask them once again to use the key words to write some true things that happened in the story. Their sentences after reading might include:

Arturo wanted to cancel the concert because he lost his baton.

Toscanini was Arturo's dog and he found the baton.

Arturo decided he didn't need a baton and he went off on a world tour.

Rivet is a very motivating way to introduce vocabulary when the words that need to be introduced are words most of your class has concepts for and some of your students have some meanings for. Children pay attention to the words as the words are being written because of the "hook" of trying to guess the word before anyone else does. They actively process the words by talking with their partners to create a sentence that uses at least two of the words and that might happen in the story. After reading, they use the words to write a sentence using at least two of the words that actually happened in the story.

Some teachers find the students are even more motivated when the teacher sets up a competition between the teacher and the class. In "Rivet versus the Class," if the students guess the word before the final letter is written, the class gets a point. If no one guesses the word before the last letter is written, the teacher gets a point. The class is always delighted when they beat the teacher, and if they guess every word, they declare it a shutout!

Providing More Opportunities for Students to Interact with Vocabulary Words

If you introduce reading vocabulary using activities such as the ones suggested in this chapter, you have taken a huge beginning step in helping children add these words to their vocabulary stores. Remember, however, that to truly own the words, students must have multiple and varied encounters with those words and they must use the words in speaking and writing. One huge obstacle to children adding these words to their vocabulary stores is that the important vocabulary for one reading selection is not apt to occur again in future reading selections. Somehow, you need to assure that your students get to interact with these words in the two or three weeks after the vocabulary was introduced. Here are some suggestions for providing those additional encounters and opportunities for students to use the words in speaking and writing.

For most of these activities you need to have your recent vocabulary words displayed somewhere in the room. You might want to set aside a bulletin board to which you can add words introduced for reading selections. Most teachers write the words they introduce on large index cards to use in their vocabulary introduction activities. Attach these index cards to your New Vocabulary Board. Continue to add words until there is no more space. Then, remove the ones that have been there and add new words in their place. When you have a few minutes, lead your students to do "sponge" activities with these words.

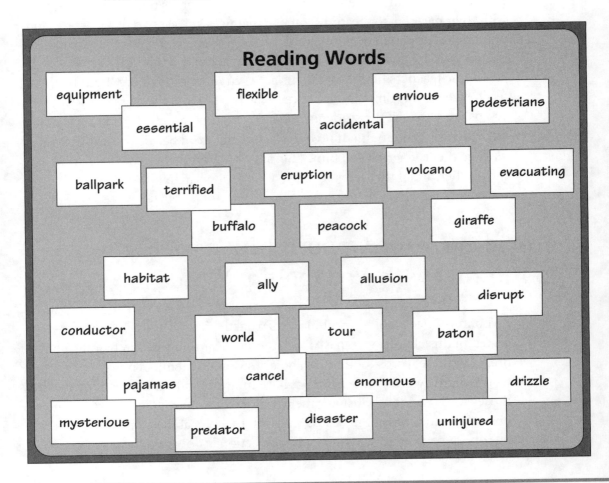

How Do These Go Together?

Have students talk with a partner and choose two words that they think go together in some way. Have them write on the front on an index card the two words that go together, then have them write on back of the card the reason they put the two words together. Let each pair of students read the two words they have chosen from the front of the card and let members of the class guess the reason they put them together. Be sure to acknowledge that there might be other good reasons for words to go together besides the reason written on the back of the card.

Front and Back of Index Cards

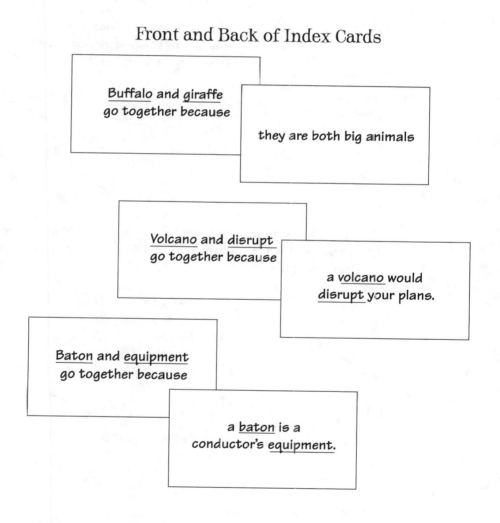

Buffalo and giraffe
go together because

they are both big animals

Volcano and disrupt
go together because

a volcano would
disrupt your plans.

Baton and equipment
go together because

a baton is a
conductor's equipment.

Word Webs

Students enjoy creating word webs (Moore, Moore, Cunningham, & Cunningham, 2006) for words they are learning. Put your students in groups and assign each group four or five of the words you have been collecting from your reading lessons. Have each group construct a web with four to six spokes. On each spoke they should put something that helps them remember the word. You may want to post a chart of possible word web categories such as the one shown on the facing page.

Two Examples of Word Webs

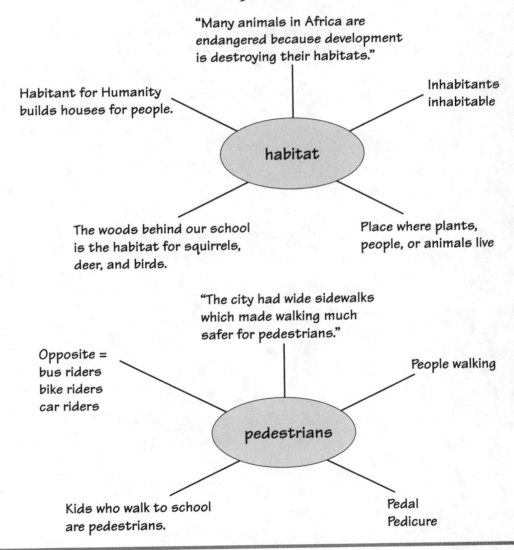

"Many animals in Africa are endangered because development is destroying their habitats."

Habitant for Humanity builds houses for people.

Inhabitants inhabitable

habitat

The woods behind our school is the habitat for squirrels, deer, and birds.

Place where plants, people, or animals live

"The city had wide sidewalks which made walking much safer for pedestrians."

Opposite = bus riders bike riders car riders

People walking

pedestrians

Kids who walk to school are pedestrians.

Pedal Pedicure

Word: **Frigid**

Category	Example
1. **Original Sentence** (Copy the sentence containing the word.)	Pat was not used to the frigid weather conditions he now faced.
2. **Dictionary Definition** (What does the dictionary say the word means?)	extremely cold
3. **New Sentence** (Use the word in a sentence that shows what it means.)	A winter day at the North Pole would be frigid.
4. **Closest Experience** (When have you seen it?)	My aunt has a big freezer, and the inside of it is frigid.
5. **Explanation of Meaning** (In your own words, what does it mean?)	Frigid means very, very cold.
6. **Main Idea** (What is it?)	a way to describe temperature
7. **Details** (What are some parts of it?)	you can see your breath, ice and snow
8. **Synonym** (What words have nearly the same meaning?)	cold, freezing, polar
9. **Antonym** (What words have nearly the opposite meaning?)	warm, hot, burning
10. **Word Family Members** (What words share the same root, or base?)	Frigidaire, refrigerator, fridge
11. **Visual** (Illustrate the meaning of the word.)	

Fill in My Blank

Have the students work together to write a sentence using one of the words. Ask them to write the sentence and underline the vocabulary word. Next, they should read the sentence aloud and have other students guess the word that goes in the blank. Students will often use more than one vocabulary word in the sentence but they should choose just one for their blank so that others can guess the word. Some sentences will follow closely the context in which students learned them, and others will use the words in different contexts. Accept whatever sentences students come up with so long as the sentences make sense.

> The plains used to be the habitat for the <u>buffalo</u>.
>
> Toscanini was the dog that found the <u>baton</u>.
>
> The people <u>evacuated</u> when the volcano erupted.
>
> We wear <u>pajamas</u> when we go to bed.
>
> My sister does yoga and is very <u>flexible</u>.

Vocabulary Bingo

Ask the students to choose 8 words to write in the 9 squares (the middle square is "free") on the Vocabulary Bingo Card. (For older students, use 24 words in 25 squares, as seen in the example.) Select words from the Vocabulary Board and give clues:

> This word means very, very frightened.
>
> This animal has beautiful feathers.
>
> This is what people do when a storm is threatening.
>
> This word means the place where an animal lives.

After each clue, have someone say the word the clue refers to and let everyone cover the word. You can play until a row is covered or until someone fills the whole card! Be sure you don't look at anyone's card as you give clues. You wouldn't want them to think you are stacking the deck!

Vocabulary Bingo

equipment	tour	pajamas	terrified	evacuating
volcano	giraffe	buffalo	baton	eruption
ally	peacock	**FREE WORD**	habitat	essential
allusion	orchestra	world	cancel	accidental
disrupt	conductor	flexible	pedestrians	envious

Guess What I Am

Students choose a word and act it out. The teacher calls on class members to guess which word the student is portraying. The person who correctly guesses gets to act out the next word. Perhaps you feel skeptical about this activity, but give it a try. Kids are less self-conscious than adults and come up with clever ways of miming the word. Children who are less verbal often delight in and excel at this activity!

20 Questions

The teacher begins this game by choosing a word and letting children ask questions that can be answered "yes" or "no." Children may continue asking questions until they get a "no." When a question gets a "no" answer, a tally mark is added to the board and the next child gets to ask a question. After 20 tally marks (20 "no" answers) the person has stumped the class. Let a child who needs to experience some success be the person to write the tally marks on the board. Here is an example:

Is your word an animal?   NO (1 tally mark)

Does your word mean really afraid?   NO (2 tally marks)

Does your word mean jealous?   NO (3 tally marks)

Does your word have 7 or more letters?   YES (Same child asks another question.)

Is your word *equipment*?   NO (4 tally marks)

Does your word describe a word?   YES (Same child asks another question.)

Is your word *flexible*?   YES!

The child who guessed *flexible* gets to choose a word and the game continues until sponge time is gone!

✿ Dump Traditional Vocabulary Introduction

Sometimes tradition is a good thing—but not for teaching vocabulary during reading lessons. We have all sat through many hours of having teachers introduce words and having students tell meanings and put words in sentences. For many of us, vocabulary instruction calls up memories of copying and memorizing definitions. When we think about it, we realize that this kind of vocabulary instruction cannot really teach students new word meanings that they will incorporate into their listening/reading/speaking/writing vocabulary stores. But the tradition is so pervasive that we often continue it without thinking about it. Vocabulary introduction does not have to be tedious and boring—for students or teachers! Buck tradition! Incorporate the activities in this chapter into your daily routine. Your students' vocabularies will grow and you and the students will look forward to vocabulary time!

chapter 5

Maximizing Vocabulary Growth During Math

Every day in every elementary classroom, teachers spend 45 to 60 minutes teaching math. Like all subject areas, math has its own vocabulary. In the early grades, this vocabulary is deceptively simple.

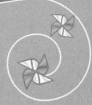

Children learn to **count forwards** and **backwards**, learn the names of the **numbers** and how to **add** them and **subtract** them, learn that a **shape** with **three sides** is a **triangle** and that a perfectly round shape is a **circle**, and learn to **measure** things, including how to measure time and money.

The bold words in the previous paragraph are the "deceptively" simple vocabulary. Often, teachers take for granted that children know the meanings of such words as **count**, **forwards**, **backwards**, **numbers**, **add**, **subtract**, **shape**, **three**, **sides**, **triangle**, **circle**, and **measure**. But many children come to school lacking these "simple" vocabulary concepts. Everyone recognizes that children who come to school with smaller-than-average vocabularies are likely to experience difficulty learning to read and write. These same small vocabularies limit children's ability to learn to do math. Explicitly teaching math vocabulary evens the playing field for all children.

This chapter will suggest ways you can incorporate vocabulary instruction as you teach your daily math lesson. When you sharpen your focus on vocabulary during math, your students will be more successful in math and their vocabularies will grow—all with no additional time or resources!

Provide Real, Hands-On Learning for Math Vocabulary

All people learn best when they have real, direct experience with whatever they are learning. Most of the vocabulary learning children do before they come to school is based in real things and real experiences. Children first learn to name things—table, chair, cat, dog, for instance. Two-year-olds delight in pointing to the objects they can see and naming them all. Put them in a new environment, such as the beach or the doctor's office, and they will almost immediately begin to point to things and ask, "What's that?" It is not only nouns that children learn through direct experience. Every young child knows the meanings of *run* and *walk* and has probably been told many times that you can't run in the parking lot! Children learn emotion words through real experiences—for example, "I know you feel sad that your friend moved away. I would be sad too if that happened."

The words we know best and remember longest are those with which we have had real, direct experience. Because effective math instruction emphasizes concrete, hands-on manipulatives, math is the perfect venue for developing vocabulary through real, direct experiences. Unfortunately, the very children whose vocabularies are most limited and who most need these hands-on experiences often attend schools where worksheets and "test prep" absorb most of the instructional time. Teachers and administrators in high-poverty schools are under such pressure to increase test scores that they may feel they can't devote time to the very experiences that would build the foundation for the success they are trying to achieve. Effective math instruction at all grade levels begins with hands-on manipulative experiences. These same experiences teach the essential vocabulary in a deep and lasting way.

Manipulate Your Students!

When providing real experiences for vocabulary development in mathematics instruction, consider your students as your first and most important manipulatives. Imagine that you wanted to build these vocabulary terms as part of a unit in geometry:

inside   outside   circle   square   triangle   corner   rectangle   sides

How could you use your children as the manipulatives to introduce these concepts? Most primary teachers have never used their children as the manipulatives, but when asked to construct an activity to teach these concepts using the children, they very quickly see how that could be done.

"I would have half the class come to the front of the room and form a circle. They would hold hands and we would make as big a circle as we could so the circle would be as round as possible. I would then ask some of the students who were not part of the circle to go inside the circle. The remainder of the class would stand outside the circle. I would get all the children to use the words **circle, inside,** and **outside** by asking questions such as, "Where is Ceretha?" "Where is Carlton?" I would have my children respond chorally in sentences:

Ceretha is inside the circle.

Carlton is outside the circle.

Next, I would choose 12 children and form them into a square. I would have them stand very close together and make clear corners. We would count the sides and decide that a square has 4 sides and the sides are the same length. We would notice and count the corners. I would have children not in the square go inside and outside the square and repeat the procedure. I would ask some of the children inside and outside to stand at the corners. To make a rectangle, I would add two more children to two opposite sides and let my children see that we still have four sides but the sides to which I added the children were longer. The triangle is simple. I would send the children on one side of the rectangle to their seats and form the remaining children into a shape with three sides and three corners.

After we had formed the shape with my directions, I would put children into groups and ask them to form the shapes in their groups. I would continue to have the children use the words to describe the shape each group had formed and count corners and sides and ask different children to stand inside or outside the shape."

Using the children as manipulatives can also work when introducing more sophisticated geometry concepts to older children. How would you use your children as the manipulatives to demonstrate the terms **circumference**, **radius**, and **diameter**? Could you arrange your students into formations to show **right**, **acute**, and **obtuse** angles?

Mathematical concepts can always be made concrete because mathematics represents the real world. Whenever possible, when introducing new math concepts and terms, consider having your students experience the concepts very concretely because they become the manipulatives.

Seek Out Real-World Examples of the Concept

After introducing the concepts by manipulating your children, write the words you introduced on index cards and engage your children in a game of I Spy. Have children chorally pronounce each word and remind them of what each word means. Children should try to use one or more of the words in their clue and then choose children to guess. Begin the game by modeling the types of clues you want them to give:

"I spy some corners on the door."

"I spy someone wearing a pin that is a circle."

"I spy a desk that is a rectangle."

Let the student who wants to answer the riddle walk and point to the object and then come up with the next riddle.

If you taught the terms **right**, **obtuse**, and **acute** angles by forming your students into these angles, can your students find any of these angles in the objects of your room? As you walk to the cafeteria or out to the playground, are there any right, obtuse, or acute angles? Does your school have a ramp that your students could observe to notice both the acute and obtuse angles formed at the bottom and top? Can your students manipulate their hands into a right angle and then turn it into an obtuse and an acute angle? Could you use pizza—or a pizza model—to teach **circumference**, **radius**, and **diameter**?

Use Manipulatives and Cut and Fold Paper

In addition to using your students as manipulatives and seeking out examples of the vocabulary terms in your school world, you can provide real experiences with various math concepts by using various objects as manipulatives. Could your students arrange popcorn or Cheerios into circles? Squares? Rectangles? Triangles? Could they place the cup that contained the popcorn or Cheerios inside and outside the shape? At the corner of the shape?

Could your older students form a right angle with popcorn or Cheerios and then manipulate it into an acute and obtuse angle? Could they form two circles, one inside the other, that had different circumferences and then place more popcorn or Cheerios inside the circles to demonstrate the diameter? Could they eat half the popcorn in the circle to turn the diameter into a radius?

Paper folding and cutting is another way to provide concrete experiences for your students with these geometry concepts. How do you fold a square to turn it into a rectangle? A triangle? How do you fold a circle to show the diameter? The radius?

Commercially produced math manipulatives are fine but if you don't have easy access to them, cereal and popcorn are nutritious alternatives and children enjoy eating their manipulatives as directed during the activity and at the end to clean up! Providing students with manipulatives to teach concepts does not have to be an expensive and time-consuming activity.

✿ Drawings and Other Visual Representations

In addition to providing a variety of real, concrete experiences with mathematics vocabulary, children can solidify their vocabulary knowledge by creating drawings and other visuals to illustrate the concept. After working with circles, rectangles, and squares and with the concepts of **inside, outside, sides,** and **corners,** children can create illustrations that show these concepts. Older children could also create illustrations of the concepts **circumference, diameter, radius,** and **right, obtuse,** and **acute angles.** Many teachers have their students record their visual representations in a math notebook. Students are allowed to represent the concepts as directly or imaginatively as they like, with the only requirement being that the vocabulary words be clearly written and correctly linked to the concept.

Other kinds of visual representation that many teachers use in math lessons are various types of charts and graphs created based on data collected. In

Illustrations Depicting Concepts

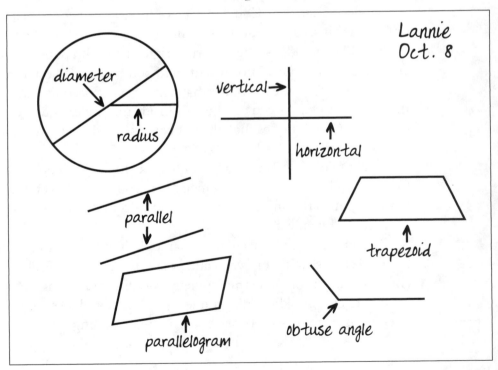

primary grades, teachers create simple bar graphs based on children's favorite colors or birthday months. Once these charts are created, they can be used to teach children comparative words such as **more**, **less**, **greater**, **most**, and **least**. Older children can strengthen their concepts of **average**, **mean**, **mode**, **median**, and **range** by graphing and labeling data based on probability experiments. Students particularly enjoy showing data in various representations if they can use the spreadsheet technology available on most school computers.

A different kind of visual representation of mathematical terms can be found in a great variety of picture books that illustrate mathematical concepts. Just as there is a wide variety of wonderful alphabet books, there is an

Our Birthday Months					
December	Josh	Joyce			
November	Ayana	Carlton			
October	Kevin M	Patrice	Jacob		
September	David				
August					
July	Grant	Kathleen			
June	Kevin C	Liz	Roberto		
May	James	Merrill			
April	Terry	Don	Zack	Scott	Ginna
March	Willy				
February	Corina	Matt			
January	Sarah				

abundance of imaginative counting books. Older children are fascinated by big numbers and will enjoy R. E. Wells's *Is a Blue Whale the Biggest Thing There Is?* (1993) and *Can You Count to a Googol?* (2000). D. M. Schwartz helps children conceptualize a million—and other enormous numbers in several books, including *If You Made a Million* (1989). David Adler has written several intriguing math books, including *How Tall? How Short? How Far Away?* Because these books have wonderful illustrations, they are often shelved with the picture books in school and public libraries. Teachers of older children often don't realize that wonderful resources for providing visual experiences to build math concepts are waiting to be discovered just down the hall!

Metropolitan Teaching and Learning publishes a delightfully illustrated series of math books for young readers tied to the National Council of Teachers of Mathematics math standards. Titles include *The Number Two, Rectangles, Spending Dimes One at a Time,* and *Fingers Go Five by Five.*

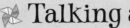 Talking and Writing

Chapter 1 included some principles for effective vocabulary instruction. The activities described so far in this chapter help you put into practice three of these principles:

- Vocabulary is learned best when it is based on real, concrete experiences.
- Pictures and other visuals help solidify word meanings.
- A set of essential words, including content vocabulary, should be directly taught.

Incorporating an activity such as List, Group, and Label and writing in math journals are ways to apply two others:

- Students develop meanings for words through multiple and varied encounters with those words.
- To truly own a word, children must use that word in speaking and writing.

List, Group, and Label

List, Group, and Label is an old strategy that was developed in the sixties by Hilda Taba (1967), an expert in concept development in social studies. I have adopted it for math as a way of having students think deeply about words and use these words in talking with one another. To do this activity, form groups of four or five children and give them a list of vocabulary words you have introduced and that you want to become part of their core math vocabulary. You can do this activity with words from just one math topic but when you have taught several topics, include words from the different topics so children can think about how they are related. This activity works best if your students can actually manipulate the words, so you may want to give them the words in a form that they can cut up into individual words. Here are the math words included when a unit on Patterns and Measurement had been taught:

cent	coin	length	width	ounce
foot	hour	gallon	short	pound
month	dime	quart	inch	yard
same	minute	mile	tall	dollar
sort	quarter	long	size	day
week	classify	different	alike	year

In this classroom, the teacher divided the class into groups of five. She instructed the groups to cut the words into columns and for each person in the group to have one column of words. Next, each student cut apart the columns of words so that each student had six words. The students were told that their job was to find words that go together in some way and pool their words to form a category, or group. Once they have combined a group of words, they should try to come up with a name or label for that group. A recorder in each student group should write down the words and the label for the group made. Then, the children should each take back their words and try to think of another group. The words in the first group can be recycled into the second group if the second group requires the words. Once students have created and labeled a second group, have the recorder record this group and label. If there is time, the students should again retrieve their words and form a third group.

When the allotted time is up—10 to 15 minutes—let each group of students share one of their word groups and tell what they called it. Here are some of the groups created by the children who worked with this list:

same, different: labeled "opposites"

week, month, year, day: labeled "things on a calendar"

ounce, pound: labeled "things you can weigh"

cent, coin, dime, quarter, dollar: labeled "money"

classify, sort: labeled "things you do with stuff"

A quick extension that really stretches their thinking can be done after the students have shared one of their groups. Give them two minutes to see if they can come up with other words not included on the list that belong in their group.

List, Group, and Label is a simple but engaging way to get your students to think about important vocabulary and to talk with one another about the attributes of each word. Children enjoy creating the groups. Thinking of the labels is hard for some children but it forces them to think about how the words go together and, working as a group, they can usually come up with an appropriate label. If you do List, Group, and Label activities periodically to review math vocabulary and give the students two minutes after they have made and shared their groups to add words to a group, you will find that they begin thinking about words they could add while making the groups.

Math Journals

When you put your students into groups to list, group, and label, you get your students talking about the vocabulary. To get them using the words in writing, many teachers incorporate key vocabulary into math journal assignments. Math journals have become popular in recent years as teachers have realized the power of having students summarize what they learn each day in a quick journal entry. Journal entries can include steps for solving various kinds of math problems, real-world examples of the math being studied, and reactions to picture books read aloud that build math concepts and math vocabulary. After being the manipulatives and using their bodies to demonstrate circle, square, rectangle, triangle, inside, outside, corner, and sides, students might be asked to write two true sentences in their journals using at least two of the vocabulary words in each sentence. Have them underline the vocabulary words to be sure they have used at least two. Once the two sentences are written, volunteers can read their sentences and the other class members can give them a "thumbs up" if the sentence is true. Here are some of the sentences written by the students. Notice that while the requirement is for two words per sentence, some students challenge themselves to use as many words as they can.

You can stand <u>inside</u> and <u>outside</u> the <u>circle</u>.

<u>Circles</u> don't have <u>sides</u> and <u>corners</u>.

<u>Rectangles</u> and <u>squares</u> have four <u>sides</u> and four <u>corners</u>.

<u>Triangles</u> have three <u>sides</u>.

<u>Circles</u> don't have <u>sides</u> and <u>corners</u> but <u>squares</u>, <u>rectangles</u>, and <u>triangles</u> have them and you can stand <u>inside</u> and <u>outside</u> all of them.

Accelerating Vocabulary Growth for English Language Learners

Numbers are the same in almost every language! The words for the numbers are different but the numerals—1, 13, 1,000, 1,000,000—are the same. Math is a subject many English language learners excel in because they recognize the numbers and can make connections to their first language. Focusing on the vocabulary of math—the specialized words used to talk about math—allows children learning English to be more successful and to learn many essential English words. Doing a variety of vocabulary activities that include real and visual experiences allows your English language learners to learn English vocabulary in the same way that young children learn most of their vocabulary words. Structuring opportunities to use the words in talking and writing provides additional experiences with the words and helps all students—especially students learning English—to develop deep and rich knowledge of the words' meanings and how they are used.

✿ The Vocabulary of Mathematics

Math contains a lot of specialized vocabulary—vocabulary specific to the subject of mathematics. Some terms such as **divisor**, **rectangle**, and **place value** are commonly used only in mathematics and children need to learn their meaning. For most children, these words are new words for new concepts. Other terms are used in math and in the non-math world with roughly the same meaning, such as **measure**, **half**, and **tally**. Because these concepts are part of the non-math world, many children have the concepts, if not the words for these concepts. These vocabulary words are examples of new words for old meanings. Another group of terms includes multimeaning words. **Prime**, **odd**, and **right** have a common non-mathematical meaning—**prime** rib, **odd** question, **right** answer—and students must learn the new (and often unrelated) meaning. In this case, they are learning new meanings for old words.

Most teachers know that they have to teach the specialized vocabulary of math for children to be successful in math. But many teachers don't realize the potential to increase the general vocabularies of their students while teaching mathematics. In this section, we will think about how you can expand students' non-math vocabulary while teaching vocabulary essential to math.

Mathematics instruction in most classrooms follows the standards and guidelines established by the National Council of Teachers of Mathematics (NCTM), which divides math instruction into five strands: Numbers and Operations, Algebra, Measurement, Geometry, and Probability. For each strand, I have created a list of the most commonly used words. The list is subdivided according to words needed in grades K through 2 and grades 3 through 5. I compiled this list by consulting the National Council of Teachers of Mathematics standards (NCTM, 2000) and the standards of several states. I also consulted the list of mathematical terms compiled by Robert Marzano and included in the Appendix of *Building Background Knowledge for Academic Achievement* (2004).

The list of basic mathematical terms is included only to show the potential for vocabulary development while teaching mathematics. Given your curriculum, there will be words you will want to add and there may be some words you will want to delete. The list includes some very common words that are important to mathematics but that may be so well known by your students that they don't deserve any instructional emphasis. The words are arbitrarily assigned to grades K through 2 or 3 through 5, and you will likely find words on one list that in your school belong on the other list. Look at the lists as a starting point for thinking about expanding your students' math and non-math vocabulary during your everyday math instruction.

Numbers and Operations

For many teachers, this is the part of the mathematics curriculum that is most familiar. Children learn to **count, add, subtract, multiply,** and **divide.** They perform these functions with **whole numbers, decimals,** and **fractions.** The essential vocabulary for this strand includes the following words:

Numbers and Operations, Grades K through 2

add	forwards	number	subtract
addition	group	odd	subtraction
backwards	half	ones	sum
count	hundred	place value	tens
difference	less	plus	total
digit	minus	regroup	whole
equal	more	rename	zero
even	none	set	

Look at the words K–2 children need to use and understand to be successful with numbers and operations. Which words are math words only? Which words have the same meaning in math as they do in general use? Which words are multimeaning words with a different meaning in math from the meaning children might already know? Do any words have word parts that might help children remember what they mean and that might help them learn how these word parts work?

For most K–2 children, the words **add, addition, sum, subtract, subtraction, digit, place value, rename,** and **regroup** are specific math terms. They are taught during math time through concrete experiences as children manipulate objects and learn to add and subtract.

Backwards, forwards, count, group, less, more, whole, half, equal, tens, ones, none, zero, hundred, and **total** are examples of words that have a general use that is very much like the mathematical use. If you teach the general meaning of these words along with the mathematical meaning, you can use the familiar meaning to connect to the mathematical meaning for children who know that meaning and you can teach the general meaning for that word for children who don't know it. To introduce the concept of **forwards** and **backwards**, for instance, you might let children move cars forwards and backwards and then make the connection to counting forwards and backwards. The concepts of **group, less,** and **more** can be taught in the non-mathematical sense by having students pile up groups of various objects and decide which group has more and which group has less. The concepts of **whole** and **half** can be developed by having children share something—an apple, a sandwich, or a piece of paper. The concepts of **zero** and **none** can be developed by relating them to a ballgame in which the final score was 5 to 0. How many points did the losing team score? None! Children hear and use the word **hundred** in their real world. Does anyone know someone who is 100 years old? Do they know that a football field is 100 yards? All these words—and many more—have a general meaning and a mathematical meaning that are very similar. By starting with the general meaning, you can quickly help extend a known concept to the world of mathematics. For any children—including English language learners who don't know the general meanings—you are teaching general vocabulary they need to know.

Some words have a general meaning that is quite different from the mathematical meaning. The words **even** and **odd**, for example, are used in phrases such as these:

"I have two and you have two. Now we're even."

"We got beat even though we played hard."

"It is odd that he is so late and he didn't call."

"I like Uncle Joe but he is a little odd."

These meanings of **even** and **odd** show very little resemblance to the mathematical use of even and odd numbers. When learning multimeaning mathematical vocabulary such as **even, odd, difference,** and **set**, children may be confused by the other meaning of the word they know. Having children access their familiar meaning of the word first and then explaining that the word has a different meaning in math staves off cognitive confusion and teaches both meanings of the word for those who don't know the more common meaning. Before teaching the term **set** in math, have children think of things that come in sets such as Legos and tea party dishes. Have children compare objects and describe the difference between them before teaching the mathematical meaning for **difference**.

Whenever you are teaching a math word that has any common word parts, seize the opportunity to help children learn how these word parts work. For the K–2 Numbers and Operations Vocabulary, you could point out that **rename** and **regroup** start with the prefix **re** and that **re** often means again. "Robert, when you replay a game, you play it again." "Anna, when you restart the computer, you start it again." **Rename** means "name again" and **regroup** means "group again." Second-graders could think about the relationships between **add/addition** and **subtract/subtraction**. Begin with some **tion** pairs they know, such as **collect/collection** and **direct/direction**. Help them see that what they have when they collect baseball cards is a baseball card collection. "Tony, when you direct someone how to go someplace, you give them directions." "Olivia, when you add, you are doing addition, and when you subtract, you are doing subtraction." You may also want to point out that when your students count backwards, they are counting back. Drawing the children's attention to word parts helps them develop deeper meanings for the vocabulary and reminds them that many big words are made up of familiar word parts.

Numbers and Operations, Grades 3 through 5

associative	division	million	product
billion	divisor	multiples	quotient
commutative	equivalent	multiplication	rational
decimal	estimation	multiply	rounding
denominator	factor	negative	thousand
distributive	fractions	numerator	trillion
divide	improper	percent	
dividend	infinite	prime	

In the upper grades, there is also math vocabulary that is specific to math, vocabulary for which the general meaning and the math meaning are closely related, and multimeaning vocabulary for which the general meaning might mislead students about the math meaning. Many of the math vocabulary words for upper grades have word parts that will help students develop a deeper meaning for the words and that will help students learn to use word parts as meaning clues to new words. From the Numbers and Operations, Grades 3 through 5 list, the following words are probably specific to math terms:

divisor quotient equivalent associative commutative thousand million billion trillion multiples multiply multiplication denominator numerator percent decimal fraction

These words need to be explicitly taught using as many real and visual experiences as you can provide. Because these are both new words and new concepts, students need to have a variety of experiences with these words, including using these words in speaking and writing.

The words **divide**, **estimation**, and **infinite** are words that have a general meaning and a math meaning that are closely related. Beginning with the general meanings that many of your students know allows you to then help them transfer their knowledge to the specific mathematical meanings.

Words whose general meaning and mathematical meaning are closely connected help students quickly acquire math vocabulary. Some words, however, have a general meaning that is not clearly related to the mathematical meaning, and if students know the general meaning, this general meaning could lead to confusion with the math concept. When introducing math words whose general meaning might lead students astray, attack the problem head on by helping students access the general meaning and then explaining that these words have a different mathematical meaning. Here are some

general meanings your students may have that will not help them learn these math terms:

dividend—stocks pay dividends
division—the automotive division
factor—many factors in making a decision
improper—improper behavior
prime—prime time
product—anything that is produced
rational—rational thinking
rounding—rounding up cattle

Words with Helpful Parts

This set of words has many words with helpful word parts. You may want students to notice that **multiply**, **multiples**, and **multiplication** all begin with the prefix **multi**, meaning "many." Other common words in which **multi** means "many" are **multitudes**, **multinational**, and **multiracial**. The words **divide**, **dividend**, **divisor**, and **division** all share the same root. The prefix **im** gives **improper** its opposite meaning, just as it does in **impossible**, **impatient**, and **imperfect**. The adjectives **associative** and **distributive** have the same root as the verbs **associate** and **distribute** and the nouns **association** and **distribution**.

Math Vocabulary for Geometry, Measurement, Algebra, and Probability

Here are the lists of common mathematical terms for the other four math strands. Just as for Numbers and Operations, use these lists as starting points for developing your list of core math vocabulary for these strands. Think about which words are specific to math and need to be taught with concrete, hands-on experiences. For which words do your students have a general meaning that will help them quickly develop the mathematical meaning? Which words are multimeaning words with a general meaning that is quite different from the mathematical meaning and that might confuse students and interfere with their understanding of the mathematical meaning? Introduce these multimeaning words by reminding students of the general meaning and explicitly teaching students that these words have different meanings in mathematics. Many words in all four strands have word parts that will help students solidify the meaning of the word and expand their vocabularies.

Geometry (K–2)

above	circle	long	short
after	cone	middle	sides
before	corner	outside	square
behind	cube	over	tall
below	direction	rectangle	top
between	inside	right	triangle
bottom	left	shape	under

Geometry (3–5)

acute	flip	plane	rotation
angle	horizontal	polygon	segment
axis	intersect	prism	slide
circumference	isosceles	pyramid	solid
congruent	obtuse	radius	sphere
cylinder	parallel	ray	symmetric
diagonal	parallelogram	reflection	transformation
diameter	pentagon	rhombus	trapezoid
equilateral	perpendicular	right (angle)	vertical

Measurement (K–2)

calendar	gallon	money	time
cent	greater	month	volume
clock	height	most	week
coin	high	nickel	weigh
compare	hour	ounce	weight
cup	inch	penny	wide
dime	least	pint	width
distance	length	pound	yard
dollar	long	quart	year
estimate	measure	quarter	
fewer	mile	seconds	
foot	minutes	temperature	

Measurement (3–5)

area	Fahrenheit	meter	perimeter
capacity	gram	metric	thermometer
Celsius	kilometer	milligram	
centimeter	liter	milliliter	
degrees	mass	millimeter	

Algebra and Patterns (K–2)

alike	first	properties	size
classify	order	same	sort
different	pattern	second	third

Algebra and Patterns (3–5)

array	diagram	inequality	proof
bar graph	equation	line graph	variable
constant	function	pie graph	

Data Analysis and Probability (K–2)

chance	graph	outcome	table
collect	organize	predict	tally

Data Analysis and Probability (3–5)

average	grid	midpoint	probability
data	mean	mode	range
function	median	model	ratio

Teaching the Academic Vocabulary of Mathematics

In his powerful book, *Building Background Knowledge for Academic Achievement*, Robert Marzano (2004) makes the case for the direct teaching of vocabulary in every subject area. He refers to content-specific words as "academic vocabulary" and argues that the enormous task of providing direct and explicit teaching of anything close to the 1,000 to 3,000 words students need to add to their vocabularies each year becomes much more reasonable if vocabulary instruction is part of every subject area every day. Furthermore, in addition to maximizing the number of words it is possible to teach well, teaching the academic vocabulary of a subject area maximizes the potential for learning in that subject area. Elementary teachers spend approximately an hour each day teaching mathematics. Across the K–5 years, that hour each day adds up to over 1,000 hours of math instruction. If just a fraction of that 1,000 hours were devoted to engaging vocabulary instruction, all children would leave elementary school with larger vocabularies and stronger mathematical concepts.

chapter 6

Maximizing Vocabulary Growth During Science

Science is another subject in the elementary curriculum that provides many opportunities for vocabulary development. Just as in math, children who become fluent with the language of science learn more science while simultaneously expanding their science and general vocabularies.

Also like math, effective science instruction includes many hands-on experiments and investigations that provide students with real, concrete experiences that provide anchors for their vocabulary knowledge. To maximize vocabulary development during science, we build on these concrete experiences, provide virtual experiences when real experiences are not possible, and use a variety of pictures and other graphic representations. Because science topics are usually pursued across several weeks of instruction, the variety and repetition required to add new vocabulary words will occur within the learning cycle as key vocabulary is used in various ways. We do want to make sure that we are structuring activities in which students use the vocabulary words in speaking and writing.

Just as for math, I compiled a list of core science vocabulary. In constructing the list, I consulted several sources, including Marzano's (2004) list of elementary science vocabulary, *National Science Education Standards* published by the National Research Council (1996), and the elementary science standards for several states. My hope is that teachers view these lists as starting points for developing their own lists. Depending on the grade level the topic is taught in your curriculum, some words may be too advanced for your students and some words may be so well known that they don't deserve any attention. If your science curriculum includes other topics not included in this list, you can develop your own list of core science vocabulary for that topic.

This chapter will describe how real, virtual, and visual experiences can anchor vocabulary development by connecting the discussion of these to specific science topics.

Provide Real, Hands-On Learning for Science Vocabulary

Experiments and investigations that engage students in real, hands-on learning need to be a part of the learning cycle for every science topic. As an example for how to maximize the potential of this concrete experience for vocabulary development, I have chosen the topic of Electricity and Magnets. Here is the list of core vocabulary I compiled for that topic. (Remember that given your grade level, curriculum, and students, you may want to add or delete words from this list.)

Electricity and Magnets

electricity	insulator	bulb	current
magnets	conductor	wire	charge
attraction	circuit	battery	static
repulsion	parallel	switch	grounded
power	series	generator	

Looking at this list of core vocabulary, it becomes immediately obvious how the hands-on experiments—testing objects to see if they are attracted or repulsed by magnets, making a light bulb light, constructing a parallel and series circuit, and other experiments—provide the concrete experiences to anchor the development of this vocabulary. Because students will be conducting these experiments in small groups, they will be talking to each other and using the vocabulary words in their discussions. Writing can occur in an uncontrived manner as children write down their predictions of which objects will be attracted to a magnet before experimenting and record their observations after experimenting. For this topic, it seems natural to have students draw and label with the appropriate words the results of some of their experiments.

Drawing and Labeling
the Results of a Science Experiment

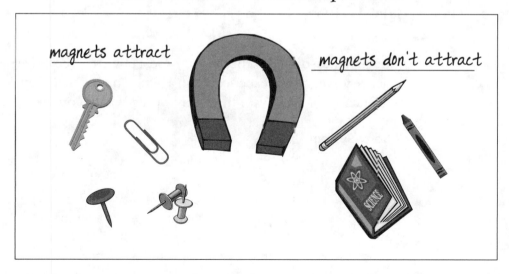

Many key concepts and vocabulary for science topics can easily be developed through hands-on experiments, but there are some more sophisticated concepts that children cannot experience directly. When the hands-on experiments have been completed, children can extend their knowledge of any science topic and vocabulary if you choose books like these for your teacher read-aloud:

- The Let's Read and Find Out Science Series (HarperCollins) includes almost 100 titles such as *Energy Makes Things Happen, Switch On, Switch Off, Floating in Space,* and *What's It Like to Be a Fish?*

- The Rookie Read About Science Series (Scholastic) includes dozens of books including *What Is Friction?, It Could Still Be a Robot,* and *What Is Electricity?*

- The Windows on Literacy Science Focus Series (National Geographic) includes hundreds of titles for young readers including *A Frog Has a Sticky Tongue, Simple Machines,* and *Magnets.*

- For older students, the Reading Expedition Science Series (National Geographic) includes titles such as *Looking at Cells, Volcanoes and Earthquakes,* and *Matter, Matter Everywhere.*

Learn Science Vocabulary through Virtual Fieldtrips

Although hands-on experiences are the most powerful vocabulary anchors, not all science topics can be experienced in a hands-on manner. Consider how you would anchor vocabulary for these core words in a unit on the Solar System.

Solar System

solar system	moon	Mercury	orbit	gravity
astronomy	Earth	Saturn	planet	shadow
sky	Mars	Uranus	revolve	comet
sun	Jupiter	universe	outer space	meteor
star	Venus	eclipse	telescope	asteroid
constellation	Neptune	rotation	atmosphere	galaxy

A few of these concepts could be developed concretely. You could have your students conduct an experiment using a flashlight and a globe and demonstrate **revolve** and **shadows**. Most of these concepts, however, are not able to be demonstrated or simulated in a classroom. This is when you are glad to be teaching in the digital age and you make plans to take your students on some virtual fieldtrips. Both the NASA website (www.nasa.gov/kids) and the Smithsonian Art and Space website (www.nasm.si.edu/) provide a huge variety of virtual exploration possibilities. Captivating videos and animations are available at Solarviews (www.solarviews.com).

The much loved Mrs. Frizzle is the "Mother of Virtual Fieldtrips." Don't miss the opportunity to read *The Magic School Bus Lost in the Solar System* by Joanna Cole to your students as part of the unit. Other Magic School Bus science books include *The Magic School Bus Plants Seeds*, *The Magic School Bus Inside the Human Body*, *The Magic School Bus on the Ocean Floor*, and *The Magic School Bus Inside the Earth*.

Using Vocabulary in Speaking and Writing

Because your students will not be doing many experiments in groups related to the topic of the Solar System, opportunities to use the vocabulary words in speaking and writing will not occur as naturally as in other subjects. You will need to contrive opportunities for your students to use the vocabulary words as they talk to each other and write.

The core vocabulary for the Solar System includes the names of the eight planets in the solar system of Earth. (Too bad about poor Pluto!) To get students talking about the planets and the features of the planets, you might put your students to work in groups and complete a data chart summarizing the most important information about these planets. (It is important that you have them complete this chart as a group because your real purpose is for them to use solar system vocabulary as they talk to one another. Completing this chart alone would not accomplish the "talk" purpose.) Encourage them to use books and other resources to find information. Once they complete the data chart as a group, have each child choose one planet and write a paragraph summarizing the information on the chart. Partner your children up and have them peer-edit each other's paragraphs.

Two of the activities described in Chapter 4 work well with science words and children enjoy doing them. To get children to talk to one another and use the vocabulary words, post the core words and have students do How Do These Go Together? and Fill in My Blank.

The Planets

Planet	Size	Distance from Sun	Atmosphere	Weather	Year	Special
Earth	Medium	Third	Nitrogen and oxygen	Moderate	365 days	Plants, animals, and people
Venus	Almost same as Earth	Second	Carbon dioxide	Hot	225 Earth days	Rotates opposite direction
Mercury	Smallest	Closest	Almost none	Hot-day Cold-night	88 Earth days	Iron core
Mars	Almost same as Earth	Fourth	Carbon dioxide	Cold	2 Earth years	Huge canyon
Uranus	Third largest	Seventh	Hydrogen and helium	Cold	84 Earth years	10 rings 15 moons
Saturn	Second largest	Sixth	Hydrogen	Cold, windy	30 Earth years	Rings made of rocks, ice, and dust
Neptune	Same as Uranus	Farthest	Hydrogen and helium	Cold, windy	165 Earth years	Visited by Voyager 2
Jupiter	Largest	Fifth	Hydrogen and helium	Cold	12 Earth years	Mostly made of gases

How Do These Go Together?   Have students talk with a partner and choose two words that they think go together in some way. Ask them to write on the front of an index card the two words that go together and the reason they put them together on the back. Let each pair of students read the two words they have chosen from the front of the card and let members of the class guess the reason they put them together. Be sure to acknowledge that there might be other good reasons for words to go together besides the reason written on the back of the card.

Fill in My Blank.   Have students work together to write a sentence using one of the words. Tell them to write the sentence and underline the vocabulary word. Ask students to read the sentence aloud and have other students

Cards for How Do These Go Together? Activity

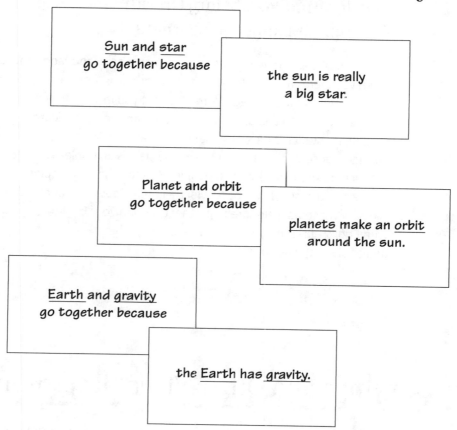

Sun and star
go together because

the sun is really
a big star.

Planet and orbit
go together because

planets make an orbit
around the sun.

Earth and gravity
go together because

the Earth has gravity.

guess the word that goes in the blank. Students will often use more than one vocabulary word in the sentence but they should choose just one for their blank so that others can guess the word. Some sentences will follow closely the context in which students learned them and others will use the words in different contexts. Accept whatever sentences students come up with as long as the sentences make sense.

Uranus is the seventh planet from the sun.

Earth and Saturn are the only planets with an atmosphere.

One year on Mars is about two Earth years.

The planet Earth holds its atmosphere because of gravity.

Venus is about the same size as Earth.

Accelerating Vocabulary Growth for English Language Learners

Think about your own experiences learning a new language. How did you feel when you were called on to speak that language in front of the whole class? Did any of your foreign language instructors put you in small groups and structure activities for you to talk using the new language you were learning? To learn new vocabulary, students must use that vocabulary in talking and writing—but trying out new vocabulary in front of the whole class is an unpleasant and anxiety-producing experience for most people. Having children complete activities with partners and in small groups provides a comfortable environment for speaking the new vocabulary. Be sure to partner or group your English language learners with English-first children who will encourage them and applaud their efforts.

Drawings and Other Visual Representations

In addition to providing a variety of real, concrete experiences with science terms, your students will develop deeper, broader meanings for key vocabulary if you make the most of all your visual resources, including picture books, pictures in your science textbook, and pictures and other visuals your students draw. Consider the power of visuals for vocabulary development for the topic of Animals.

Animals Core Vocabulary
(Include names of animals common to children's environment, such as dogs, ants, squirrels, bees, fish, etc.)

habitats	amphibians	behaviors	hibernate
birds	reptiles	features	animal
insects	fish	food	
mammals	body parts	shelter	

Animals is the most popular science taught in the elementary school. All children have some experiences with animals and most children delight in learning more about them. You will want to begin your Animals unit with those animals your children have had direct experience with and with those available in your school environment. If possible, arrange for a day when parents and other adults can bring pets to school for a pet party. Consider the possibility of adopting a class pet. Take the children on an animal-spotting walk and find as many animals as possible—including ants, spiders, birds, and squirrels—in your environment or in a nearby park. Use important vocabulary terms such as **habitat**, **shelter**, **mammals**, and **insects** in talking about these familiar animals.

Rounding up whatever real animals you can is a wonderful way to begin your unit but you will have to rely on pictures and other resources for most of your experiences. Fortunately, there are many wonderful sites on the Internet that feature animals and a plethora of picture books. Gail Gibbons, the most prolific writer of informational books about animals, has written dozens of beautifully illustrated books on animals, including *Dogs*, *Sharks*, *Penguins,* and *Horses*. Many teachers share one or two of Gail Gibbons's animal books with the whole class. Next, they form the class into groups to read her books and books by other authors about animals of their choosing. The groups gather information about the animals and may record the information on a data chart with the following categories:

Animal	Type (insect/mammal, etc.)	Habitat	Shelter	Food	Body	Behaviors

Notice that in completing this data chart the group is using and thinking about almost all the core animal vocabulary.

Many teachers have their students create an Animals book. To make sure your students are learning the key concepts and using the core vocabulary, you may want them to write a paragraph about each animal, including information about its habitat, body parts, shelter, food, and behaviors. Depending on the age of your students, you may want them to include at least one insect, reptile, amphibian, bird, fish, and mammal, as well as a diagram they draw with the body parts labeled.

Talking and Writing

If children are researching animals in groups, completing data charts, and writing about and drawing different animals, you can be sure that they are using the core vocabulary in speaking and writing. If you want to provide other opportunities, consider putting students in groups to create animal riddles and animal cinquains. Model for your students the information you want them to include in their riddles and cinquains and make sure the core vocabulary is displayed to support their writing. You may want to compile these riddles or cinquains into a class book or publish them in a class newsletter.

Reptiles

Cold blooded

Snakes, turtles, alligators

Bodies covered with scales

Reptiles

More Speaking and Writing Opportunities

Three other structures for getting your students to talk and write are particularly suited to science vocabulary. Consider how you could use Ten Important Words, Categorize, and concept charts to deepen your students' science vocabularies and provide a structure for discussion and writing.

Ten Important Words

Ten Important Words (Yopp & Yopp, 2002) is a simple but effective strategy for getting your students to think about and use key vocabulary. Children read a selection and their job is to choose the 10 most important words. (Assign them to read the selection by themselves, with partners, or in small groups, depending on the amount of support your students need with the text.) When all the children have read the selection and chosen the 10 words, a class tally is made. For each word chosen by any student or group, a tally is made of how many other people or groups chose that word. The 10 words chosen by the most students become the 10 most important words for that selection and are listed in the order of the number of times the words were chosen. After reading a selection on *Sea Turtles*, one class compiled this list of the top 10 most important words.

1. sea turtles
2. ocean
3. migrate
4. endangered
5. shells
6. flippers
7. swimmers
8. nests
9. reptiles
10. scaly

Once the top 10 list is compiled, you can engage the students in a variety of tasks that require them to talk about, write about, draw, or act out these words. Yopp and Yopp, the creators of this strategy, suggest distributing different color index cards to your students, with the color signifying what they should do with the word. Here are some possible tasks and the colors they might signify:

Green: List synonyms and antonyms.

Red: Create three good sentences that use the word in different ways.

Blue: Draw two pictures that illustrate the word.

Pink: Act out the word.

Orange: Return to the selection and find sentences and pictures in the selection that further explain the word, and put sticky notes on them.

White: Create a concept chart for the word, including examples and nonexamples.

The different colored cards are distributed to the children randomly and children with the same color gather together and choose two words they think will be well illustrated by the task their color signifies. After 10 to 15 minutes, the class reconvenes and each group shares their product with the whole class.

Ten Important Words can be used with any informational text. Depending on the length of the text and the age of your students, you may want to adjust the number (up or down) by a few words. In addition to providing your students multiple opportunities to actively engage these words, this strategy, if used regularly, will help children with the important but difficult task of identifying key vocabulary in their own reading.

Categorize

Categorize is another activity that engages children with key words they are going to read. For this activity, you decide on four or five categories and the key vocabulary that fit into those categories. Before children read a selection, they assign the words to categories. As they read they adjust the categories into which they put the words based on the knowledge gained from reading. To get your students using these words in speaking, have them work in partners or small groups to categorize and read the selection. Here are some categories and words for the *Sea Turtles* selection.

Sea Turtles

Eat	Enemies	Types	Body

black	flippers	loggerhead	scutes
carapace	green	nostrils	seaweed
crabs	hawksbill	people	sharks
eyes	jaws	plankton	shells
fish	jellyfish	plastron	whales
flatback	leatherback	ridley	

Concept Charts

Another way to help students develop a rich meaning for a term that represents a big concept is to have them create a concept chart (Frayer, Frederick, & Klausmeier, 1969). To complete this chart, students work together to come up with characteristics and examples and non-examples. Once they have filled in characteristics, examples, and non-examples, they create their own definition. Part of developing a complete meaning for a word is knowing what it is as well as what it is not. Thinking of non-examples helps students clarify and deepen the concept.

Mammals Concept Chart

Definition (own words)	Characteristics
Mammals are warm-blooded animals that drink their mother's milk, are born alive, and have hair.	Warm-blooded Drink mother's milk Have hair on their bodies Born alive

mammals

Examples	Non-Examples
dogs, horses, humans, whales, cats, chimpanzees, squirrels	sharks, fish, snakes, reptiles, insects, worms, ants, birds

Maximizing Vocabulary Development through Word Parts

English is the most morphologically complex language. Linguists estimate that for every word a person knows, there are seven other words the person could quickly connect meaning to if he or she understands how word parts—prefixes, suffixes, and roots—work together. Whenever you teach vocabulary in any subject area, ask yourself if there are other words that you could quickly teach your students by showing them the related words and talking about how the words are related. Here are just a few of the "bonus words" you could add to your students' vocabularies based on Weather, Solar System, and Animals core words. As you look at the core vocabulary lists, think about all the other words your students could quickly learn.

Science Word	Bonus Words
cloud	cloudy, cloudless
rain	rainy, raincoat, rainstorm
sun	sunny, sunshine, sunflower
snow	snowy, snowstorm
wind	windy, windless
frost	frosty, defrost
freeze	freezer, refreeze, antifreeze, froze, frozen
fog	foggy
evaporation	evaporate
storm	stormy, hailstorm, rainstorm, snowstorm
humidity	humid
pressure	press, impress, depress, compress, pressurize
thermometer	speedometer, barometer, kilometer
meteorologist	meteor, meteorology
habitat	inhabitants
amphibians	amphibious
behavior	behave
hibernate	hibernation
astronomy	astronomer, astronomical, asteroid
universe	universal
rotation	rotate
planet	planetarium, aquarium, terrarium
revolve	revolution
telescope	telescopic, microscopic
atmosphere	atmospheric

Core Vocabulary for Other Common Science Topics

Here is the core vocabulary for other common science topics. Think about the kinds of real, virtual, visual, speaking, and writing experiences you could engage your students in for maximum science learning and vocabulary development.

Weather

weather	clouds	freezing	hurricane
seasons	hot	sleet	tornado
climate	rain	hail	storm
fall	sun	ice	humidity
winter	snow	fog	high
spring	wind	precipitation	low
summer	warm	evaporation	pressure
thermometer	cool	rain gauge	barometer
temperature	cold	thunder	meteorologist
air	frost	lightning	

Plants
(Include names of plants common to children's environment, such as oak tree, grass, rose bush, hedge, etc.)

plant	leaves	seeds	air
parts	stem	needs	water
roots	flowers	light	soil

Sound

sound	vibration	music	eardrum
wave	pitch	instruments	echo
volume	high	voice	
loud	low	vocal cords	
soft	noise	microphone	

Properties of Substances/Five Senses

substances	freeze	hardness	see
senses	melt	odor	hear
solid	size	float	smell
liquid	shape	sink	taste
gas	color	solution	touch
dissolve	texture	mixture	

Animal and Plant Life Cycles/Adaptation

life cycles	metamorphosis	survival	interaction
adaptation	genetic	prey	species
egg	endangered	predator	cell
larva	extinct	diversity	organism
pupa	parent	habitat	photosynthesis
adult	offspring	prehistoric	
behavior	growth	dinosaurs	

Soil, Rocks, and Minerals

soil	clay	fossils	pebbles
rocks	silt	sedimentary	boulders
minerals	gravel	metamorphic	
sand	humus	igneous	

Ecosystems/Environment

ecosystem	environment	atmosphere	conditions
community	renewable	conservation	recycle
nonliving	nonrenewable	natural	population
pollution	fuel	resources	ozone
decompose	threatened	changes	global warming

Earth and Land Forms

crust	geological	eruption	canyon
mantle	weathering	earthquake	desert
core	landslide	glacier	ocean
erosion	flood	avalanche	formation
deposition	volcano	mountain	

Light and Energy

energy	acceleration	nuclear	forms
light	friction	solar	refraction
force	speed	radiation	reflection
inertia	mass	contract	absorption
momentum	heat	expand	

Motion and Balance

motion	gravity	pulleys	pushing
balance	machines	levers	pulling

Human Body/Nutrition/Health/Safety

body	blood	carbohydrates	doctor
nutrition	respiration	fats	physician
health	oxygen	proteins	poison
safety	digestion	symptoms	medicine
food	circulation	disease	hospital
skeleton	nutrients	infection	emergency
bones	vitamins	germs	accident
muscles	calories	virus	injury
joints	exercise	fever	
heart	weight	nurse	

✲ General Science Terms

The following terms include words for which all elementary-grade students must develop deep and full meanings. Students will have direct experiences with these words because they will do them—**describe**, **predict**, **compare**—and they will compile them—**properties**, **characteristics**, **features**. Most of these words have a general meaning that is very similar to the science meaning. A few words have a general meaning that is quite different from the science meanings and that might be confusing in the science context.

science	predict	data	experiment
scientist	describe	analyze	results
investigation	compare	communicate	similarities
properties	classify	measure	differences
characteristics	record	graph	variables
observe	collect	diagram	microscope

These words are so commonly used that some teachers might assume students know what these words mean and make the mistake of using these words without any explanation. Many students, however, do not have rich concepts for these words. You can increase their success in science and build their general vocabularies by taking a few minutes to introduce each word and help students connect the word to what they know. Many of these words have related words that share the same root. Teaching the related words helps students build fuller meanings for the target words and helps them learn to use word parts to figure out pronunciations and meanings for new words. Here are some possible general and word part connections for these important science terms.

science/scientist   A person who does science is a scientist. We are all scientists in this room when we do science. What does an artist do? A psychologist? A tourist? An organist?

investigation   In science we do investigations to find out things. Detectives and firefighters do investigations to solve crimes and figure out what caused a fire. When we do an investigation, we say we are investigating and the people doing the investigating are called investigators.

properties   In science, properties are the things we notice about something. Is it hard or soft? Heavy or light? Does it sink or float? These are all properties. There is another meaning of property you may know. We call the things that belong to a person that person's property. Your bike and book bag and video games are your property—they belong to you. The properties you observe in science about an object are that object's property—they belong to the object.

characteristics   Characteristics are like properties but we often use the term *characteristics* when we are talking about people or animals. When we read a story, the people in the story are the characters.

observe   In science, we use all our senses to observe things and figure out their properties. We call what we observe our observations and the people doing the observing are the observers.

predict   We predict in reading when we make a guess about what is going to happen in a story. We predict in science when we make a guess about what we will find out before we do an experiment. We call what we predict our predictions. If something is easy to predict, we say it is predictable. Some things—like the weather—are quite unpredictable.

describe   When we describe something, we tell what it is like—we tell its properties. If we see someone drive away after an accident, we describe the car and the people in the car to the person investigating the accident. We call what we describe a description. Sometimes, we experience something so strange that we can't describe it and we say it is indescribable.

compare   We compare things and people every day. We compare ourselves to our brother when we say we are older than our brother. We compare the weather when we say it is hotter today than it was yesterday. We compare the pizzas at two different restaurants and decide which one we like better. When we compare, we make a comparison.

classify   We classify things when we put them into groups according to certain characteristics or properties. Our class is a group that has been put together because you are all in the same grade. When we classify things, we call this their classification. Sometimes our government has put some information together that they don't want everyone to know. This information is kept secret and is called classified. When the information no longer needs to be secret, it is declassified so that everyone can read it.

record   In science, we record our observations and predictions. We record them by writing them down or making a drawing. We record information so we can save it and look at it later. Music is recorded when it is put on a tape or CD. If you miss your favorite TV program, you can record it to watch it later. We call the person or thing that does the recording the recorder.

collect   When you collect things, such as baseball cards or stamps, you put them together and call them a collection. In science we collect information about what we are studying.

data   Data is information that we observe and record. We store information on our computers in data files.

analyze   When we analyze something, we think about what it means. When we read a story, we analyze what the characters do and say to figure out what they are thinking and what they might do next. In science, we analyze our data and try to figure out what it means and predict what might happen next. When we analyze things, we call this our analysis.

communicate   We communicate when we share ideas with others. We communicate by speaking, writing, and drawing. Often we use the phone or Internet to communicate. In science, we communicate when we share our observations, predictions, and analysis with others. When we communicate, we call this communication.

measure   We measure all kinds of things. Measuring things in science is one way we observe and collect data. We call the results our measurements. Some things cannot be measured. We say they are immeasurable.

graph   Graphs are special kinds of pictures we make in math and science to record and show our data.

diagram   Diagrams help us see how things are connected. In science, we make diagrams to show the life cycle of a frog or how electricity gets to our house.

experiment   We do experiments in science to find things out. We change things and observe what happens. Drug companies do experiments with all their medicines before they put them on the market. When something has not yet been shown to be effective, we say it is experimental.

results   Results are how things turn out. We read the newspaper or watch TV in the morning to see the results of last night's ballgame. In science, results are what we have when we finish an experiment.

similarities   Similarities are how things are alike. When two things are similar, they are not exactly the same but they are very much alike. We look for similarities when we compare things.

differences Differences are the opposite of similarities. We compare things by seeing how they are alike and how they are different. In math, we use the term *difference* to mean the answer we get when we subtract one number from another number.

variables Variables are things that change or vary. When you are deciding which new shoes to buy, you think about all the variables, including style, brand, color, and cost. In science, variables are things we can change in an experiment. How much light and how much water we give plants are variables. When things are different, we say they vary. What we wear each day to school varies with the weather.

microscope Scientists use microscopes to look at very tiny things. When something is too small to see without a microscope, we say it is microscopic. Scientists use telescopes to view stars and other things that are very far away. The telescopes have telescopic lenses.

Teaching the Academic Vocabulary of Science

Look again at all the core science vocabulary included in the lists in this chapter. Where are your students going to learn these words if they don't learn them during your science instruction? A few of these words—**weather, electricity, rain**—occur in the everyday language of all your students. Other words—**thermometer, magnet, reptiles**—occur in the everyday language of some children whose parents have high levels of education. Many of these words—**friction, precipitation, mammals**—do not occur in everyday language anywhere. Think about the television programs your students watch and the movies and videos they see. Think about the books they choose to read. The term **academic vocabulary,** coined by Robert Marzano, is the perfect label for the concept of vocabulary encountered only in the academic world of schools. To be successful, children must expand their vocabulary beyond the words they will encounter in their everyday world. Teaching the academic vocabulary of science will result in gains in science learning and in the size and depth of your students' vocabularies.

chapter 7

Maximizing Vocabulary Growth During Social Studies

Social studies is an area of the elementary curriculum in which a huge amount of academic vocabulary resides.

In addition to general words—such as **community**, **continent**, and **democracy**—students need to learn a large number of people and place names—for example, **Abraham Lincoln**, **Africa**, and **Pacific Ocean**. Just as in science, some of the social studies core vocabulary is learned by many children in everyday conversations but most words occur only as children engage in learning about the history, geography, cultures, economy, and politics of the world they inhabit.

Constructing the lists of core social studies vocabulary was the most challenging task this book presented because social studies instruction is basically teaching "the world!" Believing, however, that teachers are more apt to emphasize vocabulary if they have a list of important words they know all their students need to develop rich meanings for, I developed this list, which I hope will launch teachers into developing their own core social studies vocabulary. To develop the list, I consulted Marzano's (2004) terms for General History, U.S. History, Geography, Civics, and Economics. I also consulted the *Expectations of Excellence: Curriculum Standards for Social Studies* (NCSS, 1994) and the social studies standards of several different states. All the lists are presented here. The remainder of the chapter suggests vocabulary strategies and activities that seem to work best in social studies.

✿ Social Studies Vocabulary

Families/Neighborhoods/Communities

aunt	family	mayor	similarities
brother	future	neighborhood	sister
celebrations	generation	parents	suburban
change	grandparents	past	town
city	group	police	traditions
community	grow	present	uncle
cousin	holidays	relatives	urban
customs	individuals	rituals	
differences	leaders	rural	

Citizenship

citizen	fairness	liberty	rights
citizenship	honesty	patriotism	rules
courage	integrity	pledge	sharing
determination	justice	prejudice	truth
discrimination	laws	respect	
diversity	leaders	responsibility	

Geography
(Plus names of countries and cultures being studied)

border	environment	midwest	scale
climate	forest	mountains	south
coast	geography	north	South Pole
compass	globe	North Pole	southeast
continent	grid	northeast	southwest
country	island	ocean	valley
desert	lake	peninsula	wetlands
direction	latitude	plains	west
distance	location	plateau	world
earth	longitude	region	
east	map	river	

Economics

advertising	employee	needs	spending
allowance	employer	poverty	stores
banks	export	producer	surplus
business	goods	products	taxes
buyer	import	profits	trade
competition	income	resources	training
consumer	interdependence	revenue	transportation
cost	investment	salary	unemployment
customer	job	savings	wages
debt	labor	scarcity	wants
earn	manufacturing	seller	workers
economy	money	services	

State History/Geography
(Plus important people and place names for your state)

agriculture	economy	local	state
capital	governor	population	tourism
cities	history	recreation	towns
counties	industry	region	transportation

U.S. History
(Plus important people and place names)

abolition	depression	integration	reconstruction
amendments	election	inventions	representatives
America	emancipation	judicial	reservation
assassination	equality	legislature	revolution
campaign	executive	majority	segregation
civil war	explorer	minority	senators
colonist	freedom	nation	settlers
colony	frontier	patriot	slavery
confederacy	government	pilgrims	taxes
constitution	immigrants	pioneers	union
country	independence	president	United States
democracy	Indians	railroads	vote

✿ Building Vocabulary through Real Experiences

The most striking difference between the social studies vocabulary lists and the math and science lists is the large number of words for which real, hands-on experiences cannot be provided. Social studies vocabulary is replete with abstract concepts—**citizenship**, **democracy**, and **segregation**. Even the words that are real things—**continents**, **plains**, **mountains**, and **oceans**—are not readily available to most teachers and students. Many social studies terms—such as **pilgrims**, **colonists**, and **pioneers**—existed at a prior time in history but are no longer part of our everyday experience.

The fact that many social studies concepts are not easily taught through direct experience does not change the reality that new concepts and the vocabulary words that describe those concepts are best learned through real experience. Knowing that children need direct experiences to truly own words, many teachers introduce social studies words to children using simulations and fieldtrips.

You may not think you use simulations in your teaching of social studies, but you probably do. Think of the Thanksgiving feasts primary teachers often invite parents to. Children learn about the first Thanksgiving and dress up as pilgrims or Indians to celebrate the feast. In addition to learning the obvious vocabulary—**Thanksgiving**, **pilgrims**, **Indians**, and **feast**—children begin to develop their understanding of abstract words such as **customs** and **traditions**. They connect some important social studies place names to the pilgrims who had to cross the **Atlantic Ocean** and landed at **Plymouth**, **Massachusetts**. They learn important geography terms if they locate England, Massachusetts, and the Atlantic Ocean on a **map** and a **globe**.

To introduce children to important economics concepts, many teachers transform their classrooms for a few weeks into a microworkshop. Children **manufacture** certain **products** or perform certain **services** and are paid **wages** for their **labor**. Abstract concepts such as **revenue**, **surplus**, **income**, and **taxes** are built into these classroom economic simulations.

Many elementary schools have student **governments**. **Elections** are held for the important **offices** of school **president** and **vice president**. Students in each class **vote** by secret **ballot** and **elect representatives** who become part of the school **legislature**. Some schools even have a **judicial council** that helps make school **rules** and determines how these rules will be **enforced** and **interpreted.**

When important **national** and **state elections** are being held, many schools hold mock elections. Students learn about the important **issues** and **vote** for the **candidate**s of their choice. Because of their simulated experience in **democracy**, these students eagerly watch the results of the elections and compare the state and national results with the results at their schools.

In many schools today, fieldtrips are limited by tight budgets and liability concerns. The majority of fieldtrips taken by elementary children, however, are linked to the social studies curriculum. Walks to places in your school neighborhood can make the notions of communities, community helpers, and services clearer to your students. If a visit to your state's capital or our nation's capital is out of the question, could you visit the seat of local government? Would the mayor or city manager take a few minutes to lead a tour of your local municipal building and talk about the services provided by your local government? Do you have a local museum that you and your students could visit and begin to think about history by learning about the history of your community? When thinking about how you can provide real, concrete experiences to anchor social studies concepts, always consider what fieldtrip options you have.

Direct, hands-on experience with social studies terms does not occur as naturally in social studies as it does in math and science. Knowing how important real experiences are to anchoring important vocabularies, teachers and schools that are serious about maximizing vocabulary development in social studies seek out opportunities to involve their students in simulations of the social studies concepts and maximize the learning from any possible fieldtrips. In classrooms that use simulations and an occasional fieldtrip, social studies comes alive and student motivation and engagement are greatly increased.

Virtual and Visual Experience

When you can't provide real experience, look to your virtual and visual resources to anchor abstract social studies terms. Just as you can take virtual fieldtrips in science, your class can travel to distant places and back in time using the Internet and other computer resources. One of the original virtual fieldtrips and still popular in the 5th edition is *The Oregon Trail* (The Learning Company). In this game students cross the country in a Conestoga Wagon and test their wits against the weather and a variety of realistic misfortunes. This social studies simulation game was so popular that it now has several sequels, including *The Yukon Train, The Amazon Trail,* and *The African Trail.* There are also a variety of economic simulation games, including *Lemonade Tycoon* (Hexacto) in which students set up a lemonade stand and try to make a profit. To succeed, they have to consider variables such as location, how hot the weather is, and how much of each supply to buy.

Perhaps you can't take a real fieldtrip to the White House or Plymouth Plantation or the Jamestown of John Smith, but through the Internet, you can make a virtual visit. Before investing your time and resources in a virtual fieldtrip, make sure it will be worth your while. Some sites have only pictures and text. Others have videos and interactive games to engage your students. *National Geographic* is the source of many marvelous virtual fieldtrips. Africam (www.africam.com/wildlife) will take you to many beautiful parks in Africa where your students can view wildlife on the webcam.

Pictures and other visuals can help you build social studies concepts. Photographs that represent different historical time periods are particularly useful in helping children picture life in a world very different from their own. A picture file of digital images of important people and places is invaluable in anchoring social studies vocabulary. Google and other search engines have a "search image" function that makes it remarkably easy for you to compile your picture file.

Picture Walks in Social Studies

In Chapter 4, Picture Walks were suggested for introducing vocabulary before reading. Picture Walks are a very effective way to introduce vocabulary before students read a social studies selection in a textbook or other source such as a *Weekly Reader*, *Scholastic News*, or *Time for Kids* article. When you do a Picture Walk with students, you make use of the pictures in the selection to connect new words to old concepts and to build new concepts.

Picture Books

A wide variety of picture books are another invaluable resource that directly or indirectly teach social studies content and vocabulary. Picture books can transport you and your students to locations all over the world and back in time to historic moments. Abstract terms such as **segregation**, **prejudice**, and **equality** come to life if you share David Adler's biography of *Rosa Parks* with your students. **Democracy**, **constitution**, **independence**, and many other abstract terms become real to your students if you read them Maestro and Maestro's *A More Perfect Union: The Story of the Constitution*.

National Geographic publishes several series of books that help build social studies concepts. Its Travels Across America series includes *The Northeast, The Southeast, The Midwest, The Southwest,* and *The West*. Its Windows on Literacy Social Studies series includes *The Great Pyramid, The Story of the Pony Express, Race to the Pole,* and many other wonderfully illustrated titles. David Adler's picture biographies make history come alive. Titles include *A Picture Book of George Washington, A Picture Book of Harriet Tubman, A Picture Book of Jackie Robinson,* and *A Picture Book of Lewis and Clark*.

When looking for things to read aloud to your students that will help them build concepts, look beyond biography and other factual books to poetry and fiction. Many of the wonderful poems and stories enjoyed by elementary children have geographical and historical settings that help children learn about other times and cultures and anchor core social studies vocabulary. *The Way We Do It in Japan* by Geneva Cobb Iijima is a story of a boy and his family who move to Japan for a year and experience life in a very different culture. Many adults learned a lot of geography and historical concepts about the Plains by reading the *Little House on the Prairie* books by Laura Ingalls Wilder. Social studies is the part of the curriculum in which teachers help children develop their beginning understandings of history, geography, and culture. Books can indeed be your transport back in time and across the land and seas.

Kid-Friendly Definitions

Chapter 4 contrasted dictionary definitions with kid-friendly definitions and suggested that although real, virtual, or visual experience is always required when introducing new words that are new concepts for your students, kid-friendly definitions could be used to introduce students to new words for concepts they already know. Imagine, for example, that the new vocabulary you wanted to teach in a unit on Communities included the words **past**, **present**, and **future**. You decide that most of your children have some concept for each of these words and just need to connect the new word to the old concept. You introduce each word with a student-friendly explanation and invite your children to share their connections with these words. The vocabulary introduction might sound something like this.

"Boys and girls, we are going to be learning more about our community this week and we are going to learn about how our community was different a long time ago when your grandparents were your age. We need to learn some new words to talk about the differences and this is the first word I want you to think about."

(Teacher shows the students an index card with the word **present** written on it and has everyone pronounce **present**.)

"Now I know you know one meaning for the word **present**. When would someone give you a present?

(Kids eagerly share examples of getting presents for birthdays, Christmas, etc.)

"Yes, we often get presents on our birthdays and other holidays. There is another meaning of **present** I want you to think about. **Present** can mean 'right now' or the time we are currently living in. Let me show you another word and we will think about the difference between **present** and **past**."

(Teacher shows **past** on an index card. Kids pronounce **past** and teacher reminds students of a meaning they may know for **past**.)

"Many of you know that I walk to school and I walk past the library on my way here. Who else walks to school? What things do you walk past to get here?"

(Kids share examples of walking past the store, gas station, park, and other neighborhood landmarks.)

"**Past** has another meaning. **Past** can mean something that happened a long time ago. Most of you know that before I moved here, I lived in California. I could say that in the past, I lived in California. But in the present, I do not live in California. I live here."

(Teacher asks children who lived in other places before moving here to share where they lived in the past.)

"So, **present** means right now and **past** is anytime before right now. Sometimes the past is a long time ago and sometimes it is just a little while ago. But the past is always before the present. Now let me show you another time word."

(Teacher shows **future** on an index card.)

> "This is the word **future**. Everyone say **future**. The future is a
> time that has not yet happened. I could tell you that my mom,
> who still lives in California, is thinking about moving here in
> the future. She is not presently here but she may move here
> sometime later this year—in the future. Think of something
> that has not happened yet but you think it will happen in
> the future."

(Children share examples of future events—including the impending
birth of a baby sister, a planned trip to Iowa, and the retirement of a
grandfather. Teacher shows all three index cards, has the students
pronounce the words again, and expands the kid-friendly
definitions.)

> "So when we talk about what is happening right now, we call
> that time the **present**. If something happened before this time,
> we call that the **past**. Sometimes the past is just a little while ago
> and sometimes the past is a long time ago. When something has
> not happened yet but we are waiting for it to happen, we say it
> will happen in the **future**."

With any type of vocabulary introduction, it is crucial that students have
a chance to use the word for which the teacher had just provided an explanation. The easiest way to assure that your students are actively involved in your
vocabulary introduction is to seat them with a talking partner and have them
"turn and talk." After providing your student-friendly explanations for **past**,
present, and **future**, have them connect their experiences to these words by
giving them a "turn and talk" task.

> "Turn and talk to your partner about something important
> happening right now in your life, something that happened in the
> past, and something you are looking forward to happening in the
> future. Be sure to use the words **present**, **past**, and **future** so your
> partner will know when the things you are talking about happened."

Give them a minute to talk and then ask the children to tell something their
partners told them. Prompt them to use the words **past**, **present**, and **future**
in their sharing.

"Paul, can you tell us something Manuel told you that happened in the past?"

"Carla, can you tell us something Miguel told you that will happen in the future?"

"Sharon, can you tell us something Kevin told you that is happening now, in the present?"

Even in social studies where many of the words are new words for new concepts, some vocabulary words are simply new words for concepts your students already have. When you are introducing vocabulary such as **past**, **present**, and **future** that most of your students already have concepts for, you can give them kid-friendly definitions for those words and then provide an opportunity for them to connect each word to their experience by giving them a quick "turn and talk" task. If you regularly ask children to share what their partner told them, they will listen better to each other in anticipation of needing to share that information with the class.

🌀 Maximizing Vocabulary Development with Multimeaning Words and Word Parts

The vocabulary you build during social studies will help your students build richer social studies concepts. Just as in other subject areas, some words you teach will have the same meaning in general use as they have in social studies. Other words have a social studies meaning and another different meaning. If students know the more general meaning of a term, that meaning can confuse them and interfere with comprehension when they are reading social studies content. Helping students access the more general meaning for the word and then explaining how the word has a different meaning in social studies can prevent confusion. For children who don't know the word's general meaning, your teaching of both meanings will help them add two new meanings to their vocabulary store.

Another way to increase vocabulary size when teaching social studies words is to draw their attention to word parts—prefixes, suffixes, and roots. Whenever you teach vocabulary in any subject area, ask yourself if there are other words that you could quickly teach your students by showing them the related words and talking about how the words are related. Here are just a few of the "bonus words" you could add to your students' vocabularies if you teach other meanings of a multimeaning word and capitalize on word parts.

Social Studies Word	Related Words	Other Meaning
border	borderless, borderline	Borders bookstore
coast	coastline, coastal	coast down the hill coaster under a glass
continent	continental, intercontinental	Continental Airlines
direction	direct, director, misdirected	director of a play
east	eastern, easterly, southeast, northeast, mideast	
planes		airplanes
scale		scale that weighs things fish scales scale a mountain
consumer	consume, consumable	
competition	compete, competitive, competitor	
depression	depress, antidepressants	
prejudice	judge, judicial, judiciary, justice	
nation	national, nationality, nationalize, international, internationalize	
product	produce, producer, production, reproduce, reproduction	answer in multiplication
courage	courageous, encourage, encouragement, discourage	
rights	rightful	right answer right turn
responsibility	responsible, irresponsible	
economy	economical, economics	economy car
population	popular, overpopulated	
patriotism	patriot, patriotic	New England football team

✿ Talking and Writing

After words are introduced in as vivid and rich way as possible, students need opportunities to use these words as they talk and write. Students will eagerly discuss social studies words if their task is to List, Group, and Label, create word webs and concept maps, choose 10 important words, and categorize.

List, Group, and Label

Chapter 5 described how you could use a List, Group, and Label activity to help your students interact with and develop deeper meanings for math words. The List, Group, and Label activity format was actually developed to promote concept development in social studies. Here is how you could use List, Group, and Label to get your students talking the new social studies vocabulary.

- Create a list of social studies words with which you want students to work. The list can include words only from a topic you are currently studying or can include words from several topics.

- Form groups of four or five children and give them the list of vocabulary words you have chosen. Have them cut the words apart so that each child has an equal number of the words.

- Have the groups of students work together to put words into groups that go together in some way. Once they have combined a group of words, they should come up with a name or label for that group.

- Appoint a recorder in each student group who will write down the words and the label for the group made.

- Once one group is made and recorded, have the children take back their words and create a new group. Students should come up with a label for this second group and the recorder should record the group and the label.

- If there is time, have the students create, label, and record a third group.

- When the allotted time is up—10 to 15 minutes—let each group of students share one of their word groups and tell what they called it.
- If there is time, have students choose one of the word groups they made and come up with other words not included on the list that belong in their group.

Here are some important social studies terms and how some students categorized the words into groups.

governor	nation	president	state	mayor
judge	ballot	past	town	city
Indians	community	country	future	county
pilgrims	urban	present	colonists	capital
rural	products	workers	suburban	council
leaders	election	tourism	factory	government

rural, urban, suburban—labeled "different parts of the county"

future, past, present—labeled "time words"

workers, leaders, colonists, pilgrims, Indians, governor, president, judge, mayor—labeled "people"

colonists, pilgrims, Indians—labeled "people who aren't here any more"

governor, government—labeled "words with govern as part of them"

List, Group, and Label is a simple but engaging way to get your students to think about important vocabulary and to talk with one another about the attributes of each word. Children enjoy creating the groups. As they create the groups, they are talking with one another about the words and how they fit together. Many students particularly like the final activity in which they choose one of their groups and try to come up with words that were not on the list that belong in that group.

Word Webs

Chapter 4 described how students can create vocabulary word webs by drawing a web with four to six spokes and filling the spokes by choosing from various word categories. Be sure you make this a group activity because your

Word Web

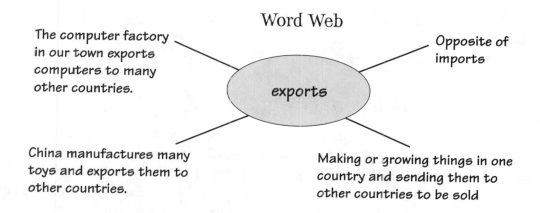

The computer factory in our town exports computers to many other countries.

Opposite of imports

China manufactures many toys and exports them to other countries.

Making or growing things in one country and sending them to other countries to be sold

students will use the vocabulary words in talking and listening as they decide which categories to include in their web.

Concept Charts

In social studies, we often help students learn about character traits such as responsibility, courage, and honesty. After the students have talked about

Courage Concept Chart

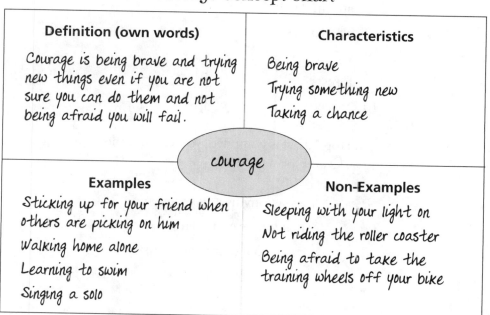

Definition (own words)

Courage is being brave and trying new things even if you are not sure you can do them and not being afraid you will fail.

Characteristics

Being brave
Trying something new
Taking a chance

courage

Examples

Sticking up for your friend when others are picking on him
Walking home alone
Learning to swim
Singing a solo

Non-Examples

Sleeping with your light on
Not riding the roller coaster
Being afraid to take the training wheels off your bike

these concepts, they can work in groups to create concept charts. Concept charts always include non-examples as well as examples that help students clarify an abstract concept.

Ten Important Words

Ten Important Words was described in the science chapter (Chapter 6) and is equally effective in social studies. Children read a selection and their job is to choose the 10 (or 8 or 12) most important words. When all the children have read the selection and chosen the 10 words, a class tally is made. The 10 words chosen by the most students become the 10 most important words for that selection and are listed in the order of the number of times the words were chosen. After reading a selection on *Japan*, one class compiled this list of the top 10 most important words.

1. Japan
2. Asia
3. Tokyo
4. islands
5. Pacific Ocean
6. automobiles
7. electronics
8. volcanoes
9. forests
10. soccer

Once the top 10 list is compiled, you can use the colored index cards to signify tasks and form groups.

Green: List synonyms and antonyms.

Red: Create three good sentences that use the word in different ways.

Blue: Draw two pictures that illustrate the word.

Pink: Act out the word.

Orange: Return to the selection and find sentences and pictures that further explain the word and put sticky notes on them.

White: Create a concept chart for the word, including examples and non-examples.

After 10 to 15 minutes, the class reconvenes and each group shares their product with the whole class.

Categorize

Categorize is another activity that was described in the previous chapter and that works equally well in social studies. Here are the categories and words one teacher chose for a selection on Japan.

Japan

Food	Geography	Products	Sports

Asia   sumo   ships   Pacific Ocean   karate
fish   automobiles   tea   soccer   rice
mountains   forests   baseball   textiles   soybeans
robots   noodles   islands   electronics

❈ Teaching the Academic Vocabulary of Social Studies

Look again at all the core science vocabulary included in the lists in this chapter. Where are your students going to learn these words if they don't learn them during your social studies instruction? A few of these words—

Accelerating Vocabulary Growth
for English Language Learners

Because many social studies terms are abstract, they present special problems for children who are learning English. Much of the academic vocabulary of social studies does not consist of just new words for known concepts. Both the concept and the word are apt to be unknown. Unlike many science and math words, you often cannot ask your English language learners to tell you the word for the new concept in their language because they lack both the word and the concept.

The difficulty of teaching social studies vocabulary to English language learners is further complicated by the fact that these students often lack the cultural referents many native English speakers have for the words. Children who associate Florida with Disneyworld and New York with the New York Yankees have some kind of starting point for thinking about these states, the northeast, the southeast, and the Atlantic Ocean. Using as much real, virtual, and visual experience as possible and providing varied opportunities to use new vocabulary in speaking and writing is important for all vocabulary learning. Assuring these multiple, interactive encounters with words is essential for your English language learners to master social studies vocabulary.

workers, **holiday**, **family**—occur in the everyday language of all your students. Other words—**honesty**, **traditions**, **election**—occur in the everyday language of some children whose parents have high levels of education. Many of these words—**region**, **scarcity**, **imports**—do not occur in everyday language anywhere. Think about the television programs your students watch and the movies and videos they see. Think about the books they choose to read. Social studies, like all subject areas, has an academic vocabulary that children must learn. Much social studies vocabulary is abstract. Providing your students with multiple real, virtual, visual, speaking, and writing encounters with the academic vocabulary of social studies will result in greater social studies learning and increases in both the size and depth of your students' vocabularies.

chapter **8**

Maximizing Vocabulary Growth During Art, Music, and Physical Education

T o truly make vocabulary development a priority, you must seize every opportunity across the school day to expand and enhance your students' vocabularies.

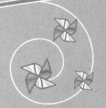

This chapter explores some often overlooked vocabulary development opportunities in the gym, on the playground, and in the art and music rooms. Just as for other curriculum areas, your first step toward maximizing vocabulary growth during art, music, and physical education is to create a list of core words for these topics. To develop this list, I consulted Marzano's (2004) Physical Education, Arts, Theatre, Dance, and Music lists and the curriculum standards of several states for these areas. Consider these lists as starting points for developing your own list.

Physical Education

ability	endurance	offense	skate
activity	equipment	opponent	skiing
amateur	exercise	pass	skill
athlete	field	physical	skipping
balance	fitness	player	slide
baseball	flexibility	practice	soccer
basketball	football	procedure	softball
catch	gallop	professional	sport
challenge	game	race	sportsmanship
championship	goal	racket	stretch
climb	gymnasium	recreation	strike
coach	gymnastics	referee	swimming
competition	hockey	relay	tennis
course	hopping	rink	throw
court	jogging	rules	track
cycling	jump	running	training
defense	kick	score	umpire
diving	league	shoot	winners
dribble	movement	sideline	

Music, Dance, and Drama

actor	drums	musician	role
applause	duet	orchestra	scale
audience	entertain	percussion	scenery
band	guitar	performance	solo
bass	harmony	performer	song
cast	horn	piano	soprano
clapping	instrument	pitch	stage
composer	keyboard	play	strings
conductor	lighting	production	tempo
costume	march	props	tenor
dance	melody	recorder	theater
drama	music	rhythm	voice

Visual Arts

artist	contrast	kiln	perspective
brush	crayon	materials	scissors
camera	draw	medium	sculpture
canvas	easel	museum	texture
clay	exhibit	oil	tools
color	gallery	paint	watercolor

Develop Vocabulary through Real, Concrete Experiences

As you look at the lists, did all the opportunities for real, hands-on experiences jump out at you? If social studies contains the largest number of abstract words and concepts, the arts and physical education contain the largest number of concrete words. Your students "do" most of these words: They sing and dance and jump and draw and paint. The things they don't do are things they touch, hold, and use—such as basketballs, paintbrushes, and recorders—or things they help create—for example, scenery and costumes. There are a few abstract terms—**rules**, **harmony**, and **perspective**—but these abstract terms can quickly be connected to concrete experiences.

One very potent reason for spotlighting vocabulary during art, music, and physical education is that the experiences that provide the most powerful way to learn new words is the essence of what these curriculum areas are all about. You don't need to contrive any real experiences; you just need to capitalize on them and draw attention to the words that name and describe the activities. The challenge for you in developing vocabulary as you engage your students in art, music, and physical education activities is that vocabulary development opportunities are so obvious that you will overlook them! That is why developing your core vocabulary lists for these areas is so important. Post your list somewhere where you will glance at it often. As you lead your students in activities, be sure you use all the appropriate words and give your students opportunities to use them. Write the words on index cards, as you do for other subject areas, and have your students pronounce the words and use them with one another.

Before going to the playground, for instance, show the students the word **equipment** and ask them what equipment the physical education helpers need to carry to the playground. Take a few seconds to expand the meaning of **equipment** by asking them what equipment is needed for various tasks, such as cooking, fishing, and camping. Ask them to turn and talk to a partner about some activity they do on the weekend and what equipment they use for that activity.

Before giving out instruments for your rhythm band, show students the word **instruments**. Have them pronounce the word and then name the instruments used in the rhythm band. Ask the children to name any instruments they know about that are not rhythm band instruments. Who do they know who plays the guitar? The drums? The piano? Where have they seen an organ? A keyboard? Ask them to think about their favorite instrument and why it is their favorite and then turn and talk to their partner about their favorite instrument.

As you begin your art activity, show students the words **medium** and **materials**. Talk about the different materials that are used in art and the different mediums (media) they have worked in this year. Show them the materials they will use today and what medium they will work in. Give the children just a minute to imagine that they grow up to become great artists and decide which materials and mediums they will be famous for. Then ask them to turn and talk about their artistic aspirations.

Real experiences are what art, music, and physical education are about. You don't need to contrive the experiences to teach the vocabulary—you just need to make sure you don't miss the opportunity!

Develop Vocabulary through Virtual and Visual Experiences

In addition to being musicians, artists, and athletes, most people are spectators at these events. Discuss with your students how people go to **galleries** and **museums** and see **exhibits** by a variety of **artists** using a variety of **media**. If taking your students on a fieldtrip to a gallery or museum is not feasible, could you set up an exhibit and transform your classroom or halls into a gallery? PBS and the Discovery Channel produce some excellent videos that you can use to take your students on virtual fieldtrips to see the greatest art all over the world. As you and your students take these virtual voyages, be sure to seize all the vocabulary development opportunities, including learning the names of the most famous artists and the names of places where they created their art and where that art is displayed.

Would it be possible to take your students to a concert? Would your local high school band come to your school and put on a concert for your students? Does your faculty and school staff contain any musicians who shouldn't give up their day job but who could put on a concert for your students? If you can't arrange any kind of real musical event for your students, you could surely find some video footage of bands and orchestras. Be sure you connect all the vocabulary words possible to whatever musical experiences you arrange for your students to watch. In addition to the obvious words—**musician**, **orchestra**, **band**, **conductor**, **concert**, and names of instruments—seize the opportunity to develop other concert-related words such as **audience**, **applause**, **intermission**, and **solo**.

Could you take your students to a sports event? Perhaps a local intramural game? Can you use some video of a game to build sports-related vocabulary? Look at the list of physical education vocabulary and imagine the possibilities to develop vocabulary, including vocabulary that is not just sports specific—for example, **competition**, **endurance**, **defense**, **offense**, and **professional**.

In addition to engaging your students in doing art, music, and physical education, you have numerous opportunities to engage your students as spectators for art, music, and sports events. Make the most of these virtual and visual opportunities to develop arts- and sports-specific vocabulary as well as vocabulary with more general use. Most kids love art, music, and physical education. If you connect vocabulary development to these activities, some of that positive affect might translate into more positive attitudes toward words!

Accelerating Vocabulary Growth for English Language Learners

Have you noticed that there are no language barriers when your students participate in art, music, and physical education activities? Take advantage of the "level playing field" all your students are on during these activities to spotlight vocabulary. All students will benefit and your English language learners will absorb the words as they participate fully in the activities.

⚝ Capitalize on Student Enthusiasm for Art, Music, and Physical Education to Teach Word Parts

Look again at the lists that began this chapter. Many of the words—even the simple, common words—have word parts used in other (and often more complex) words. Simple words such as **jog**, **dance**, **skate**, **paint**, and **drum** can be used to teach the **er** meaning that transforms these simple words into **jogger**, **dancer**, **skater**, **painter**, and **drummer**. **Actor** and **conductor** can be used to demonstrate that sometimes **or** at the end of words indicates a person who does the action. Here are some words you can help your students build meaning for by demonstrating how many other words are related to art, music, and physical education words.

Arts/Physical Education Words	Bonus Words
jog/dance/skate/ paint/drum, and others	jogger/dancer/skater/painter/drummer and others
ability	able, unable, inability, disability
activity/actor	act, active, inactive, action, react, reaction, counteract
athlete	athletic
competition	compete, competitive, competitor
cycling	bicycle, tricycle, unicycle, motorcycle, cyclist
defense/offense	defend/offend, defensive/offensive
endurance	endure, unendurable
flexibility	flex, flexible, inflexible, reflex
sportsmanship/ championship	friendship, fellowship
composer	compose, composition, decompose, decomposition
conductor	conduct, conduction

(continued)

Arts/Physical Education Words	Bonus Words
entertain	entertainer, entertainment
harmony	harmonious, harmoniously, disharmony
production	produce, producer, reproduce, reproduction
scenery	scene, scenic
exhibit	exhibition, exhibitor
color	coloring, discolored, colorize, watercolor
field	outfield, infield, fielder, fieldhand
movement	move, movers, immovable
drama	dramatic, dramatize
sculpture	sculptor

❋ Talking and Writing

In spite of the fact that most art, music, and physical education words are easily connected to real, virtual, and visual experiences you are providing, students still need to use the words to own them. Students would enjoy categorizing some of these words in a List, Group, and Label format.

artist	brush	canvas	draw	paint
contrast	kiln	clay	sculpture	perspective
sculptor	camera	color	crayons	easel
materials	medium	museum	gallery	watercolor
exhibit	texture	scissors	tools	oils

sculptor, artist—labeled "people who do art"

museum, exhibit, gallery—labeled "places you see art"

easel, paint, brush—labeled "equipment you need to paint with"

clay, kiln—labeled "things you need to make pottery"

Perhaps the students could complete a data chart contrasting some sports.

	Basketball	Football	Baseball	Hockey	Tennis
Equipment					
Positions					
Number of players					
Team Name					
Actions/ Movements					
Scoring					

Students also could write cinquains about their favorite sport, musical instrument, or artist.

Basketball

Shoot   baskets

Dribbling,   passing,   jumping

Bounces   off   the   rim

Victory!

Perhaps most consistent with the nature of art, music, and physical education, your students could pantomime words and have the class guess the word they are dramatizing. Imagine the fun your students will have and the good discussion that will go on as they work in groups to plan pantomimes for this list of words:

gymnastics	coach	defense	tennis
referee	equipment	relay	softball
dribble	flexibility	stretch	
balance	offense	winners	

Use Art, Music, and Physical Education to Maximize Vocabulary Learning in Your Classroom

Most of us have never thought about using art, music, and physical education as a venue for vocabulary development. When you think about the importance of providing real, virtual, and visual experiences to anchor words and when you consider students' enthusiasm for these subjects, the vocabulary connection seems obvious. In fact, I hope you will conclude as I have concluded: "How not?"

chapter 9

Words Are Wonderful!

> Being curious about the meaning of an unknown word is a hallmark
> of those who develop large vocabularies. Students become interested
> and enthusiastic about words when instruction is rich and lively.
>
> —Beck, McKeown, & Kucan, 2002, p. 13

Making vocabulary instruction and activities as engaging and lively
as possible has been one of my top priorities in writing this book.

Children enjoy listening for the words in Three Read-Aloud Words and getting to shout, "Stop! *Catastrophe*!" when you read a text where **catastrophe** occurs. They are intrigued by the sports articles you read to them and use to engage them in thinking about word parts. Their eyes are riveted to the board as you slowly write the letters of a word and they try to be the first one to guess the word you are writing. Introducing vocabulary with real, virtual, or visual experiences is important not only because this kind of experience is how children learn words best but also because they respond enthusiastically to these experiences. Talking with classmates to group words, create word webs, and plan pantomimes are social opportunities most children enjoy. Promoting a "Words Are Wonderful!" attitude has been a hidden agenda throughout this book because ultimately the attitudes your students develop toward vocabulary will determine how many new words and meanings they add to their vocabulary stores. Most of the new words students acquire as they go through school will be words they meet in their reading and develop meanings for using pictures, context, and word parts. It is not enough to know how to figure out the meanings of new words that are encountered while reading. The children have to want to do it! In addition to the suggestions in previous chapters for making vocabulary instruction as engaging as possible, here are some other suggestions for promoting word wonder.

Model Your Word Wonder During Teacher Read-Aloud

Reading aloud to your students every day is critical to vocabulary growth because children who are exposed to lots of wonderful and various books and magazines are motivated to do more independent reading. Chapter 2 suggested that including a Three Read-Aloud Words lesson each week would teach children how to use pictures, context, and word parts to figure out the meanings of new words. You can get more vocabulary mileage from your read-aloud time if you stop occasionally and marvel at the wonderful choice of words the author used. In *The Bridge to Terebithia*, Katherine Patterson (1977) describes a happy feeling as "joy jiggling inside" (p. 101).

Pausing for just a moment, rereading the phrase, and marveling at how the words let you feel what the characters are feeling help your students become aware of the power of words and how great authors choose words to paint pictures and bring you into the story. In addition, each time you stop, reread, and marvel, you are demonstrating to your students that you think words are truly wonderful.

Some books call special attention to words by presenting them in humorous or unusual ways. Countless children have delighted in Amelia Bedelia's literal attempts to dress a chicken and draw the drapes. *Donovan's Word Jar* (DeGross, 1994) is a story about a boy who becomes fascinated with words and starts collecting unusual words by writing them on slips of paper and sticking them in his word jar. Many teachers read this book to their students and then present their students with word jars for their word collections. In other classrooms, the class has a word jar. Children who find words so good they don't want to forget them jot them down on a colored strip of paper, initial them, and put them in the jar. From time to time, the words in the jar get dumped out and the person who contributed that word explains why it is such a wonderful word.

The classic read-aloud book that teachers read aloud to promote word wonder is Norton Juster's *The Phantom Tollbooth* (1961). With the Spelling Bee, the watchdog Tock, and the Humbug, Milo, the main character in *The Phantom Tollbooth,* journeys through Dictioanapolis, feasting on square meals and synonym buns. Older elementary children delight in this fantasy and find the word play truly awesome. Sharing books with children that celebrate and play with words is just one more way to show your students you are a genuine word lover.

Classroom Word Jar

Here are just a few of the many books that highlight words and word play:

Brian Wildsmith's Amazing World of Words by Brian Wildsmith

Double Trouble in Walla Walla by Andrew Clements

Tangle Town by Kurt Cyrus

Night Knight by Harriet Ziefert

All the Amelia Bedelia books by Peggy Parrish

The King Who Rained, A Chocolate Moose for Dinner, and other books by Fred Gwynn

Model Choosing Wonderful Words for Your Budding Authors

After modeling your wonder at the awesome words authors choose to paint pictures and put the reader right into the action, capitalize on your students' enthusiasm for "just the right word" by modeling how they, as authors, can use truly awesome words in their writing. Teach some mini-lessons in which you use boring, common, not-very-descriptive words in your first draft and then, noticing these "tired" words, revise your draft by replacing the "dead" words with more "lively" ones.

Don't tell the children your intent ahead of time. Just write a piece as you normally write during a writing mini-lesson. When you finish your draft, have the class read it with you and ask them if they can think of any ways you can make your writing even better. If no one suggests replacing some of your "overused" words, you will need to suggest it yourself.

> "I notice that I have some common words here that don't create very vivid pictures. **Good**, for example, doesn't even begin to describe how wonderful the cookies were. I think I will cross out **good** and replace it with **scrumptious**."

Continue replacing some of your boring, overused, or inexact words, eliciting suggestions from your students about which words need replacing and what words to use in replacing them.

Once you have modeled replacing boring words with more lively words in several mini-lessons, ask your students to try this revising strategy in one of their pieces. Have them work in partners as you circulate, giving help as needed. When they have had a few minutes to revise, select a few good examples of revision to share with the whole class.

"Show, don't tell" is a basic guideline for good writing. Unfortunately, many children (and adults) are not sure what this guideline means. To teach your students what it means, you have to practice what you preach and *show* them how to "Show, don't tell" instead of taking the far easier road of *telling* them to "Show, don't tell"!

To teach children to replace "telling" words with words and sentences that "show," write some pieces in which you purposely tell rather than show and then revise these pieces in mini-lessons with the children's help. You might also want to use paragraphs from some of your students' favorite authors as examples and rewrite these by replacing the showing words with telling words and sentences. After identifying the places where your students wish the writer had shown them rather than told them, read the original to them and compare the "telling" version with the "showing" version. After several mini-lessons, partner your students and ask them to help each other find examples in their own writing where they could make the writing come alive by replacing some of their telling words with showing words and sentences.

❀ Use "Stuff" to Build Vocabulary and Promote Word Wonder

Everybody likes stuff! Look around your house or apartment and identify common objects your students might not know the names of—even if they have the same objects in their houses! Here are some of the objects one teacher brought to school for "show and talk."

> vases in assorted sizes, colors, and shapes
>
> *balls*—tennis ball, baseball, basketball, football, golf ball, volleyball, and beach ball
>
> *art*—watercolors, oils, and photographs in frames of different colors, materials, and sizes
>
> *kitchen implements*—turkey baster, strainer, spatula, whisk, and zester
>
> *tools*—hammer, screwdriver, nails, screws, drill, and wrench

In addition to the names of objects, of course, lots of descriptive words are used in talking about what you do with the objects. You may want to engage your students in a game of 20 Questions, in which you think of one of the objects and they see how many questions they have to ask you to narrow down which one it is.

In addition to gathering objects from home and carting them to school, look around your school environment and think about what objects your students might not know the names for. They probably know the words **door** and **window**, but can they tell you that what goes around the door and window is the **frame**? Can they tell you that the "things" that allow the door to open and close are the **hinges** and that the thing you grab to open and close the door is the **knob**? They can turn the water in the sink off and on but do they know they use **faucets** to do that? Is your playground covered with **asphalt**? **Gravel**? **Grass**? **Sand**? What kind of **equipment** do you have in your **gymnasium** and what can you do with it?

Many of the objects you bring to school or identify in school to build vocabularies can also be found in the home environments of your students. Get in the habit of posing questions that will send students looking for and identifying similar objects in their homes.

> Do you have tools (kitchen implements, balls, vases, picture frames, etc.) in your house? What do they look like? What do you use them for?

> How many faucets (hinges, knobs, ledges, door frames, etc.) do you have in your house? Count them and bring in the number tomorrow. We will add up all the numbers at the beginning of math.

> Is there gravel (asphalt, grass, sand, etc.) anywhere in your neighborhood?

> Is there a playground or park near your house? What kind of equipment does it have?

In addition to having children identify common objects in their home environments, encourage them to talk with family members about these. "Tell your family that we have these at school too and what these things are for. Tell them about how we are using batteries—like the ones you have at home—to learn about electricity."

Teachers are always looking for opportunities to make home–school connections. Having children take new vocabulary words they are learning into their home environments helps make school learning more relevant and extends each child's opportunities for vocabulary development.

❋ Encourage Your Students to Build Word Collections

Kids like to collect stuff—baseball cards, rocks, shells, and stickers, to name just a few. Find ways to enable your students to collect words and provide opportunities for them to share their collections with other collectors.

This chapter began with suggestions for promoting word wonder by including some books in your teacher read-aloud in which words are cherished. Collecting words in a jar, just as Donovan did in *Donovan's Word Jar,* is a simple way to motivate all your students to collect words.

Another simple way to establish the routine of word collecting is to have one child each day contribute a word to the One Wonderful Word board. Divide one of your bulletin boards into spaces for each student. Make each space large enough to display a large index card and label each space with each child's initials. Include a space for yourself. Each day, working in order across and down the board, one child places an index card with his or her "wonderful word" and explains why he or she chose that word. Depending on the age of your students, you may want to specify a minimum number of letters the word must have. If you like, you can also let the designated child choose three words added by other children and explain why she or he likes these words, too. When you and each child have added the first word to the board, begin the rotation again and have each child tack the second word on top of the first word. If you begin this early in the year, your students will have been introduced to 150 or more words that their classmates think are wonderful! More importantly, your students will always be on the lookout for a wonderful word so they can impress everyone with their choice. Establishing and maintaining a One Wonderful Word board takes minimal time and preparation but pays big dividends by keeping the notion of wonderful words front and center in your classroom.

Many teachers like students to keep vocabulary notebooks. If you do this, make sure your students see themselves as word collectors rather than definition copiers. In fact, most teachers do not allow students to copy any definitions into their notebooks. Rather, the students include the sentence in which they found the word and a personal connection with the word. Students often enjoy illustrating the words in their collections with pictures and diagrams. Some older word sleuths like to include some information about the word's origin.

One Wonderful Word

Mrs. C outstanding	**AC** chimpanzee	**GH** precarious	**PJM** persistent	**DM** drawbridge
BE generous	**TW** expedition	**KB** ridiculous	**JD** environment	**PLM** emergency
AM hibernate	**RA** immigrants	**SJM** generation	**BJ** firecrackers	**ZC** victorious
RS explorers	**PD** performers	**JH** video games	**SAM** delicious	**JM** championship
DC invention	**KC** brontosaurus	**DH** impressive	**CH** revolution	**KL** frustration

✿ Make Friends with the Dictionary

Think back to your elementary school days and recall your associations with the word **vocabulary**. Do you remember looking up words and copying their definitions? If the word had several definitions, did you copy the first one or the shortest one? Did you ever look up a word and still not know what the word meant because you didn't understand the meaning of other words in the definition? Did you copy that definition and memorize it for the test in spite of not understanding it? Do you remember weekly vocabulary tests in which you had to write definitions for words and use these words in sentences?

Copying and memorizing definitions has been and remains the most common vocabulary activity in schools. It is done at all levels and in all subjects. This definition copying and memorizing continues in spite of research that shows definitional approaches to vocabulary instruction increase children's ability to define words but have no effect on reading comprehension

(Bauman, Kame'enui, & Ash, 2003). Beck, McKeown, and Kucan (2002) sum up the damper that typical dictionary activities can put on word wonder.

> Becoming interested and aware of words is not a likely outcome from the way instruction is typically handled, which is to have students look up definitions. Asking students to look up words in the dictionary and use them in a sentence is a stereotypical example of what students find uninteresting in school. (p. 12)

There are, however, a variety of ways to promote active use of the dictionary that help students broaden their concepts and also teach students what a valuable resource the dictionary is. Students should learn to turn to the dictionary when they need a precise definition of a word. A teacher who regularly says, "Let's see what the dictionary can tell us about this word," and sends one child to look it up models the way adults who use the dictionary actually use it. (Did you ever see an adult look up a word to copy and memorize the definition? Maybe the reason so few adults use dictionaries is because that is the only way they ever saw anyone use it!) If you have a dictionary on your classroom computers, model how useful this is by asking a child to "see what our computer dictionary has to say about this word."

In many classrooms, helpers are appointed to jobs each week. Someone greets visitors and waters the plants. Why not appoint a weekly Dictionary Disciple? This person gets possession of "the book" and is always ready to be dispatched to the farthest corners of the wide world of words to seek and share facts about words.

Another activity students enjoy that teaches them how to use dictionaries authentically is based on the notion of semantic gradients (Greenwood & Flanigan, 2007). As described in an article in *The Reading Teacher*, semantic gradients are used to help students discern shades of meaning. Students are given a gradient with two opposites placed on each end. One example from this article has the gradient bounded by **despondent** and **euphoric**.

Despondent _____ **Euphoric**

Students are provided a word box from which they choose words to place along the gradient. For **despondent** and **euphoric**, the example words in the word box are **happy, elated, unhappy, glum**, and **sad**. Students work in groups to place these words along the gradient from **despondent** to **euphoric**. The completed gradient might look like this:

despondent   glum   sad   unhappy   happy   elated   euphoric

Students then come together as a class to share their thinking in deciding where to place the words. The authors suggest that when students become good at completing a gradient when they have a box of words to choose from, they can be given the gradient with the extreme examples of the opposites and, without the help of a word box, come up with words and place them along the gradient.

I am quite taken with the semantic gradient idea because I think children would enjoy talking about the words and trying to decide what shades of meaning they have, but I worry that many children would not have enough knowledge of the shades of meaning to make reasonable decisions. I have adapted this activity to include the students working with a dictionary and thesaurus to aid in making their decisions, thus making the task more "do-able" for more students and providing authentic experiences with the dictionary and thesaurus. I call this activity Rank Opposites. In Rank Opposites, students use a dictionary to help them decide where to put the boxed words. When students become more sophisticated at using the dictionary to decide where to place the boxed words, students are not given any boxed words. Rather, they use a thesaurus to determine which words to add and where to place them. Depending on the age and vocabulary sophistication of your students, you can vary the format, type, and number of words used. Here are some Rank Opposites variations.

One variation is to give the students the extremes placed on the continuum and six to eight boxed words. Students use dictionaries to find the words, read the definitions together, and decide where to place the words.

wail _____ guffaw

| laugh | giggle | whimper | smile |
| sob | cry | chuckle | frown |

petrified _____ fearless

| fearful | timid | afraid | courageous |
| daring | terrified | brave | valiant |

sizzling _____ frigid

| cold | lukewarm | hot | cool |
| warm | frosty | scorching | chilly |

In another version, you place the common opposites on the gradient and students decide where to place the others, including the extremes.

_____ big _____ little _____

| colossal | huge | tiny | miniature |
| enormous | gigantic | small | mammoth |

_____ like _____ dislike _____

| hate | despise | adore | worship |
| loathe | love | detest | enjoy |

Another possibility is to place one word in the center and then have students place other words to show some variation on this word.

_____ said _____

| whispered | yelled | murmured | mumbled |
| shouted | screamed | hollered | |

_____ walk _____

| scurry | saunter | stroll | sprint |
| dash | run | meander | mosey |

After students learn how to use the dictionary and determine shades of meaning, you can help them learn to use a thesaurus by providing them with the basic words but no box of words. Students brainstorm words they know with similar meanings and then look up these words in a thesaurus to come up with other examples. Given the common opposites **wet** and **dry**, students might construct a gradient that looks like this:

drenched   soaked   soggy   damp   wet   dry   arid   parched   waterless

Given the extreme opposites, **wealthy** and **destitute**, students might use the thesaurus to construct this gradient:

wealthy   prosperous   affluent   well-off   rich   poor   broke   penniless   destitute

Given the common word, **wonderful**, students might construct this gradient:

good   nice   pleasant   great   wonderful   splendid   fantastic   magnificent   awesome

For all Rank Opposites lessons, it is important for students to work in small groups to determine the words and the ranks. Remember that "talking the words" is one of the major avenues for claiming ownership of new vocabulary. When students are using shades of meaning to rank words, they will not always be in agreement. What is important is not the exact order of the words but that students are talking and thinking about shades of meaning. Be sure to communicate to your students that their thought and discussion about where to place the words—not the exact placement—is what matters.

Let Your Students Act Up!

Word dramatizations are powerful ways to help students build vivid word meanings. Both skits and pantomimes can be used to help students "get into words." To prepare your students to do vocabulary skits, select six words and write them on index cards. Tell your students that in a few minutes, their group will plan a skit—a quick little play—to demonstrate the word they have been given. Choose a few students to work with you and model for them how to plan a skit. Talk with your group as the rest of the class listens in. Plan a scene in which you can use the word several times. When you have a plan, act out your skit using the target word as many times as possible. Have one member of your group hold up the word every time it occurs in the skit.

Imagine, for example, that the word your group is acting out is **curious**. You decide that the skit will involve a dad and his 2-year-old walking to the post office. The dad and the toddler meet several people on their walk, and each time, the 2-year-old stops, points to the stranger, and asks questions:

"What's your name?"
"Where are you going?"
"What's that?"
"What are you doing?"
"What's in the bag?"
"Why are you wearing that funny hat?"

The dad smiles each time and explains to the stranger that his son is curious about everything. The strangers answer the boy's questions and then remark, "He's the most curious kid I ever saw," as they walk on.

Perform the skit as the class watches. At the end of the skit, have the people in the skit ask the audience how the skit showed that the little boy was curious. Finally, ask if anyone in the audience has a story to share about a curious person.

Next, assign the class to five groups, putting one of the children who helped in the skit in each of the groups. This child gives each group a card on which the word the group will dramatize is written. Today, the teacher is focusing on adjectives and has given the groups the words **nervous**, **frantic**, **impatient**, **jubilant**, and **serene**. The groups plan their skits with a little help from the teacher, who circulates around and coaches them. As she hoped would happen, the teacher is happy to see that the child in each group who helped in the skit is taking a leadership role and helping boost the group's confidence that they can do this.

Each skit is acted out with one person in each group holding up the card each time the word is used. The group then asks the audience what they saw in the skit that made the word "come alive." The teacher asks if anyone in the class wants to share a personal experience with the target word. After the last skit, the teacher places the six word cards with others on a board labeled "Get Your Adjectives Here! Cool Describing Words to Spice Up Your Talk and Writing."

Another form of dramatization is pantomime, which is particularly useful when the words you want to teach are emotions or actions. Imagine that you want to introduce the emotional adjectives **confused**, **disappointed**, **furious**, and **frightened**. A pair of students can be assigned to each word. The rest of the class watches the pairs pantomiming the words and tries to guess which pair is acting out each word. The same kind of pantomime can be done with actions such as **swaggered**, **crept**, **sauntered**, and **scurried**. Adverbs are fun to pantomime. Imagine four pairs of students walking to school. One pair walks **briskly**. One pair walks **cautiously**. One pair walks **proudly**. One pair walks **forlornly**.

For any kind of dramatization, it is important to conclude the activity by asking all the students to relate the word acted out to their own experience:

"When have you been confused? Disappointed? Furious? Frantic?"

"When have you swaggered? Crept? Sauntered? Scurried?"

"When would you walk briskly? Cautiously? Proudly? Forlornly?"

Acting out words in skits and pantomimes provides students with real experience with many words. They remember these words because of this real experience and because they enjoy acting and watching their friends act. Keep a list of words your class encounters that could be acted out in skits or pantomimes and schedule 20 minutes for vocabulary drama each week. You will be amazed at how their vocabularies and enthusiasm for words will grow.

Teach Children to Monitor Their Vocabulary Knowledge

One of the first steps in learning anything is recognizing that you don't already know it. Children need to notice when they come to words they don't have meanings for. Sometimes, young children get so focused on pronouncing new words that they fail to realize they don't know what it means. Children can be taught to self-assess their vocabulary knowledge using a simple scale like this one:

1 = I never heard of that word.

2 = I heard the word but I don't know what it means.

3 = I think I know what that word means.

4 = I'm sure I know what that word means.

5 = I can make a good sentence with that word.

This scale could be used with any of the activities for teaching vocabulary. To make this quick and easy, consider using a five-finger, every-pupil-response system. Say the word you are focusing on and ask everyone to show you the appropriate number of fingers. When you are focusing on words for the first time, be sure that you positively acknowledge all the responses so that children don't get in the habit of showing you five fingers just so they "look good." Try acknowledging their vocabulary self-assessment with comments such as these:

"I see lots of one and two fingers. That makes me happy because I know I chose a word you need when I chose **desperate**. **Desperate** is an important word and lots of you don't know it yet."

"Some of you think you know the meaning of **desperate** and some of you are sure you do. Can someone tell me what you think it means?"

"I see someone with five fingers up. Todd, tell me your sentence that shows the meaning of **desperate**."

After you have worked with the new vocabulary words for several days, ask the children again to show you how well they know the meanings of these words and comment on how many people are showing four or five fingers. Many teachers display a chart such as the one shown here to help children remember the five-finger vocabulary self-assessment system.

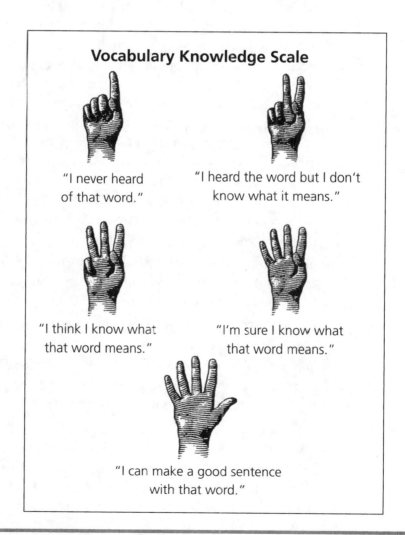

Vocabulary Knowledge Scale

"I never heard of that word."

"I heard the word but I don't know what it means."

"I think I know what that word means."

"I'm sure I know what that word means."

"I can make a good sentence with that word."

✤ Play Games

Kids love games and there are a lot of wonderful word games. Camille Blachowicz and Peter Fisher (2004) have a wonderful list of possible games. Here is my adaptation of their list:

- *Match, Go Fish,* and *Old Teacher:* Match is a card game like Concentration in which children pick up cards and take them if they have a "match." Children can construct the cards to go in the game. Match can be used to review vocabulary words taught in any area and the cards can match in different ways. Matching cards could be a picture and the word that goes with the picture (*buffalo, giraffe, peacock*); synonyms in which one word is a "tired, overused word" and the other word is a more vivid word (*happy, joyous; said, shouted; shook, trembled*); or antonyms (*even, odd; large, small; less, more; above, below*). Cards are turned over and then placed back in the same spot if they do not match. If a player gets a match, he or she takes the pair and has another turn. When all the cards have been taken, the person with the most cards is the winner. The same deck of cards that was created for Match can be used to play Go Fish. Add a card with a drawn picture of an "Old Teacher" and play a variation of Old Maid. Kids choose cards from one another and match pairs. The person left with the Old Teacher loses!

- *WORDO:* This variation of Bingo was described in Chapter 4. Choose nine words and tell the students to write them in different places on their WORDO sheet. Give definitions for words and the students cover them. The first person with a row or column covered wins!

- *Commercial Games:* Many commercial word games are appropriate for classroom use, particularly with intermediate-aged children. Popular commercial word games include Scrabble, Probe, Pictionary, Boggle, and Outburst. Newer word games are always being developed, so be on the lookout and be the first classroom in your hall to have the new, hot game!

- *Crossword Puzzles:* There are many books of simple crossword puzzles that your children will enjoy solving. Have them work together with a partner or in a trio to ensure lots of talk about the words. Several Internet sites allow you to download crossword-puzzle–creating programs.

Older children enjoy creating crossword puzzles with unit or story vocabulary. Let everyone work in small groups to create a puzzle and then let other groups solve the puzzles.

- *Computer Word Play:* Many Internet sites provide a variety of word play games and activities. Just search for word-play or word games and you will find some sites that are particularly appropriate for your students.

Use Word Humor

A man sits down at a bar and orders a club soda. He hears a soft voice say, "My, you are a handsome man." He looks around and does not see anyone else at the bar. He picks up his drink and hears, "That shirt is a good color on you." The voice seems to be coming from a bowl of nuts at the end of the bar. He calls the bartender over and tells him he thinks he is hearing voices. The bartender says, "It's the nuts. They're complimentary!" (paraphrased from Stahl and Nagy, 2006, p. 147)

Many jokes, like this one, turn on the meaning—or in this case, the two different meanings—of a word. All children enjoy jokes, even the corny jokes. Using jokes in your classroom will promote your students' "words are wonderful" attitude and provide everyone a much needed moment of comic relief. Jokes are everywhere.

Riddles are another kind of word humor. The ones that follow are from the Teaching English as a Second Language site (http://iteslj.org/c/jokes-riddles.html) but there are numerous other sites on the Internet with jokes and riddles appropriate for elementary children.

Why couldn't Cinderella be a good soccer player?
> She lost her shoe, she ran away from the ball, and her coach was a pumpkin.

What starts with E, ends with E, and only has one letter?
> An envelope.

What travels around the world and stays in a corner?
> A stamp.

What did the ocean say to the beach?

Nothing, it just waved!

What has many keys but can't open any doors?

A piano.

Which room has no doors and no windows?

A mushroom.

A man rode into town on Tuesday. Two days later he rode home on Tuesday. How is this possible?

His horse's name is Tuesday.

Which is faster, heat or cold?

Heat, because you can catch a cold.

Why are baseball stadiums so cool?

There is a fan in every seat.

Promote Word Wonder

Enthusiasm is contagious! Teachers who are enthusiastic about words project that enthusiasm by conveying their eagerness to learn unfamiliar words and by sharing fascinating words they encounter outside the classroom. Young children are usually enthusiastic about new words, repeating them over and over, enjoying the sound of language and marveling at the meanings being expressed. Encourage the continuation of this natural enthusiasm. Open your class to wondering about words, to spontaneous questions about unfamiliar words, to judgments about the sounds and values of words. Make engaging activities like the ones described in this book a regular part of everyday life in your classroom and your students will conclude that words are indeed wonderful!

Book Study Guide
for
What Really Matters in Vocabulary

Book Study Guidelines

Reading, reacting, and interacting with others about a book is one of the ways many of us process new information. Book studies are a common feature in many school districts because they recognize the power of collaborative learning. The intent of a book study is to provide a supportive context for accessing new ideas and affirming best practices already in place. Marching through the questions in a lockstep fashion could result in the mechanical processing of information; it is more beneficial to select specific questions to focus on and give them the attention they deserve.

One possibility to structure your book discussion of *What Really Matters in Vocabulary* is to use the Reading Reaction Sheet on page 194. Following this format, make a copy for each group member. Next, select a different facilitator for each chapter. The facilitator will act as the official note taker and be responsible for moving the discussion along. He or she begins by explaining that the first question is provided to start the group discussion. The remaining three questions are to be generated by the group. The facilitator can ask each person to identify at least one question and then let the group choose the three they want to cover, or the facilitator can put the participants into three groups, with each group responsible for identifying one question. The three questions are shared for all to hear (and write down), and then discussion of Question 1 commences. The facilitator paces the discussion so the most relevant information for that group is brought out. Since many school districts require documentation for book studies, the facilitator could file the sheet with the appropriate person as well as distribute a copy to all group members for their notes.

Another possibility is to use the guiding questions for each chapter. You could have the same facilitator for all chapters. Perhaps this would be someone who read the book first and suggested it to the group. Or the facilitator role could rotate. It is suggested that the facilitator not only pace the group through the questions to hit on the most important information for the group's needs, but he or she should take notes for later distribution to group members and/or administrators if required for documentation.

The provided questions are meant to provoke discussion and might lead the group into areas not addressed in the questions. That is wonderful! The importance of a book study is to move the members along in their understanding of the book content. If time is limited, the facilitator might select certain questions from the list for the initial focus of the discussion, allowing other questions as time permits.

Of course, a third option is to combine the two structures. Select the format that best fits your group and the time frame you have set for completion of the book.

All book sessions should end with a purpose for reading the next chapter. It could be to generate questions the group still has, to find implications for each person's own teaching, or to identify new ideas. Purpose setting is a time-honored way to help readers (of any age) approach the text. If you are using the questions that accompany each chapter, direct the participants to read the questions prior to reading the chapter. This will provide a framework for processing the information in the chapter.

Book Study Questions for Each Chapter

chapter 1: Why Vocabulary Matters

1. What strategies from this chapter do you see yourself using? Why?
2. Generate a question this chapter caused you to wonder about. Bring it to the group for discussion.
3. Cunningham describes an "Ah-ha!" moment about children's meaning vocabulary store. She also describes what she did to help build vocabulary. Describe something specific you have done to develop vocabulary that is consistent with the principles presented in this book.
4. Cunningham explains the difficulties inherent in determining vocabulary size. What if you could know exactly what each student's vocabulary size was? What would you do differently in your classroom? Why?
5. Are you a "word wonder" person—someone who loves to learn new words and notices words in everyday life? How do you know? How do you develop word wonder among your students? What do you think the role of word wonder is in developing vocabulary?
6. Think back to your school years. How did teachers introduce words to you? How effective was that? If one of those teachers were sitting here today, what would you say to that teacher?
7. While you were reading the description of upcoming chapters, which sounded the most intriguing? Why? What do you expect to learn there?

chapter 2: Maximizing Vocabulary Growth from Reading

1. What strategies from this chapter do you see yourself using? Why?

2. Generate a question this chapter caused you to wonder about. Bring it to the group for discussion.

3. Share personal examples of students who read a lot and had large vocabulary stores and students who read little and had small vocabulary stores. Did you teach them differently? How?

4. Do you read to your class at least once each day? Why? What are some of your read-aloud goals?

5. How do you identify what your students' reading interests are? How do you use that information when planning instruction? Why?

6. For an upcoming piece you are going to read aloud to your students, choose "Three Read-Aloud Words" and do that lesson. Share how it went and what you would change, keep, or expand.

7. Do your students read materials of their own choosing each day? Why is that a part of your day? What do you struggle with? What is easy?

8. Do you confer with your students about their reading choices? What do you struggle with? What is easy?

9. What are the ways you have your students share their choice reading? Why do you do it that way?

10. What evidence do you have of children learning new words from your read-alouds and/or their choice reading? How could you gather evidence if you don't already?

chapter 3: Maximizing Vocabulary Development by Teaching Word Parts

1. What strategies from this chapter do you see yourself using? Why?

2. Generate a question this chapter caused you to wonder about. Bring it to the group for discussion.

3. English is a very complex language. It's a wonder anyone ever learns it! Have you ever tried to explain to students why, as an example, cars "collide" but they have a "collision"? Do you ever wonder if words such as *cower, coward,* and *cow* (as a verb) are related? Share some word relationships (or nonrelationships) that surprised you.

4. This chapter on word parts addresses four areas: compound words, prefixes, suffixes, and roots/bases. Which are you most successful with? Why? How do you teach it? Which of the four do you find hardest to teach? Why?

5. Given your responses as a group to Question 4, what resources would help you teach word parts better? Why do you believe that to be the case?

6. Morpheme study can be great fun to build word knowledge and word wonder. Describe one successful activity you have done. Why do you think it works?

7. Which of the activities in this chapter have you previously used? How successful were they? Which new activities do you plan to use? Why?

8. Set a timer for one minute. Each participant should write down all the forms of or words using the word part for these words: *stand* and *probable*. Compare lists. Discuss how helpful knowing the base word is for knowing the meaning of the derived words.

chapter 4: Maximizing Vocabulary Growth During Reading Lessons

1. What strategies from this chapter do you see yourself using? Why?

2. Generate a question this chapter caused you to wonder about. Bring it to the group for discussion.

3. After describing traditional reading vocabulary instruction (introduce, one-time exposure, copy definitions, and memorize definitions), Cunningham raises the question at the beginning of Chapter 4, "How effective is this traditional reading vocabulary instruction?" What would you say to her to either counter or support her contention?

4. In the same section as in Question 3, Cunningham challenges you to think of another way to teach children who don't already know word meanings. What have you done differently? Describe your experiences teaching vocabulary during the reading lesson.

5. How does "being picky" with words you choose ("Goldilocks" words) mesh with the preselected words in the basal reading series? What alternatives do you have?

6. Read an upcoming selection in your basal reading series. Make a list of 8 to 10 words for this selection. Compare them to the words chosen by the series authors. Explain reasons for the discrepancies.

7. Bring the words from Question 6 to this group. Go through the words as Cunningham did with *equipment, flexible,* and *essential.* As a group, generate "real experiences" for the words on your list.

8. For the same list of words chosen in Question 6, develop kid-friendly definitions you can share with your students.

9. Try a Rivet lesson and share your experiences. What did you learn that you might do differently another time? Why?

chapter 5: Maximizing Vocabulary Growth During Math

1. What strategies from this chapter do you see yourself using? Why?
2. Generate a question this chapter caused you to wonder about. Bring it to the group for discussion.
3. Are your students currently keeping mathematics notebooks? Why? How do they differ from mathematics journals described later in this chapter?
4. If you are using mathematics notebooks, bring some to share with the group. Describe how they work, how long it takes, and other logistics that might help someone who has never tried either.
5. List-Group-Label is a kind of word sort. Try it with upcoming vocabulary and describe the experience at the next group meeting.
6. If you have not previously used mathematics journals, try them for at least a week prior to the next book club meeting. Describe your experience, students' learning, and your perception of the goals and values of mathematics journals.
7. Using your mathematics text and state/district standards, list the vocabulary students must know to understand the mathematical concepts at your grade level. Circle the words that have different meanings in other content areas so you can make connections for your students. Share these with your book club group so you can refine them.

chapter 6: Maximizing Vocabulary Growth During Science

1. What strategies from this chapter do you see yourself using? Why?
2. Generate a question this chapter caused you to wonder about. Bring it to the group for discussion.
3. Using your science text and state/district standards, list the vocabulary students must know to understand the science concepts at your grade level. Circle the words that have different meanings in other content areas so you can make connections for your students. Share these with your book club group so you can refine the definitions you will use.
4. Using the list of upcoming science vocabulary, discuss which specific activity(ies) from this chapter you are going to use to teach the words and why. At the next book club meeting describe the lesson(s).
5. Mathematics and science vocabulary can be much more "hands on" than much of the vocabulary in your reading series. Discuss the implications and applications of doing hands-on mathematics and science. What is the level of vocabulary processing? How do you know?

6. There are many semantic (word meaning) mapping strategies. Choose 3 words from your list from Question 3 and try one of the semantic mapping strategies yourself or with a group. What did you learn that will help you present the strategy and/or words to students? What might they struggle with in this strategy? What can you do to intervene?

chapter 7: Maximizing Vocabulary Growth During Social Studies

1. What strategies from this chapter do you see yourself using? Why?
2. Generate a question this chapter caused you to wonder about. Bring it to the group for discussion.
3. What are the implications for social studies vocabulary instruction if, as Cunningham states, these words are "replete with abstract concepts"?
4. Adults know concepts such as "citizenship" and "interdependence." How did you learn social studies vocabulary? Describe your memories.
5. Develop a list of social studies words for your grade-level concepts using texts and state/district standards. Circle those for which you could provide real-life or virtual experiences. What would those experiences look like?
6. Try "Ten Important Words" with an upcoming reading selection in your social studies text. At the next book club meeting, describe the lesson and what you learned while doing it.
7. Many of us learned abstract concepts like "freedom," "community," and so forth from reading about those concepts in historical fiction books. Using your word list from Question 5, match vocabulary with appropriate children's or adolescents' literature books.
8. Many social studies vocabulary words have multiple meanings. Put a star next to them on your list and discuss how you will target some of them in an upcoming lesson.

chapter 8: Maximizing Vocabulary Growth During Art, Music, and Physical Education

1. What strategies from this chapter do you see yourself using? Why?
2. Generate a question this chapter caused you to wonder about. Bring it to the group for discussion.
3. One of the wonderful things about a vocabulary focus during art, music, and physical education is that typically students view instruction differently in these content areas. Often there is more movement, use of specialized equipment, and a more relaxed stance. Teachers can take advantage of that atmosphere to focus on vocabulary. Discuss the pros and cons of this perspective.

4. Using the various lists of content vocabulary from previous chapters, use three colors of highlighters to mark those words that have meaning also in art, music, and physical education. For each, indicate how you can make the connection for students.

5. Which of the strategies from previous chapters would be especially apropos to each of the three content areas in this chapter? How could you help the art, music, and physical education teachers so they could use those strategies?

chapter 9:   Words Are Wonderful!

1. What strategies from this chapter do you see yourself using? Why?

2. Generate a question this chapter caused you to wonder about. Bring it to the group for discussion.

3. Have you created a "word wonder" classroom? How do you know? What do you do? Would your students say that you love words?

4. Do you have a favorite word-play activity or book? Share the activity or book with the group and explain why and how you use it.

5. Which of the activities in this chapter have you used regularly? Why? What was the response of your students?

6. Is the learning justified for the amount of time word-wonder activities take? Discuss the issue of pressure for achievement versus learning to enjoy word study.

7. In the questions for Chapter 1, you were asked if you are a "word wonder" person. Has your answer to that question changed here at the end of the book? Why?

Reading Reaction Sheet

Facilitator/Recorder (person who initiated the discussion): _____

Group reactants: _____

_____

Date of reaction/discussion: _____

Chapter title and author(s): _____

_____

Question #1: What ideas and information from this chapter could be used in classroom instruction?

Reactions:

Question #2: _____

_____

Reactions:

Question #3: _____

_____

Reactions:

Question #4: _____

_____

Reactions:

References

Anglin, J. M. (1993). *Vocabulary development: A morphological analysis. Monographs of the Society for Research in Child Development, 58* (10, Serial #238).

Artley, S. A. (1975). Good teachers of reading—Who are they? *The Reading Teacher, 23,* 285–303.

Bauman, J. F., Kame'enui, E. J., & Ash, G. E. (2003). Research on vocabulary instruction: Voltaire redux. In J. Flood, D. Lapp, J. R. Squire & J. M. Jensen (Eds.), *Handbook of research on teaching the English language arts* (2nd ed., pp.752–785). Mahwah, NJ: Erlbaum.

Bauman, J. F., Ware, D., & Carr Edwards, E. (2007). "Bumping into spicy, tasty words that catch your tongue": A formative experiment on vocabulary instruction. *The Reading Teacher, 61,* 108–122.

Beck, I. L., McKeown, M. G., & Kucan, L. (2002). *Bringing words to life.* New York: Guilford.

Biemiller, A. (2004). Teaching vocabulary in the primary grades. In J. F. Baumann & E. J. Kame'enui (Eds.), *Vocabulary instruction* (pp. 28–40). New York: Guilford.

Blachowicz, C. L., & Fisher, P. (2004). Keep the "fun" in fundamental: Encouraging word awareness and incidental word learning in the classroom through word play. In J. F. Baumann & E. J. Kame'enui (Eds.), *Vocabulary instruction* (pp. 28–40). New York: Guilford.

Clay, M. M. (1991). Introducing a new storybook to young readers. *The Reading Teacher, 45,* 264–273.

Cummins, J. (1994). The acquisition of English as a second language. In K. Spangen-berg-Urbschat & R. Pritchard (Eds.), *Kids come in all languages: Reading instruction for all students* (pp. 36–62). Newark, DE: International Reading Association.

Frayer, D., Frederick, W. C., & Klausmeier, H. J. (1969). *A schema for testing the level of cognitive mastery.* Madison: Wisconsin Center for Educational Research.

Graves, M. F. (2004). Teaching prefixes: As good as it gets? In J. F. Baumann & E. J. Kame'enui (Eds.), *Vocabulary instruction* (pp. 81–99). New York: Guilford.

Graves, M. F. (2006). *The vocabulary book.* Newark, DE: International Reading Association.

Greenwood, S. C., & Flanigan, K. (2007). Overlapping vocabulary and comprehension: Context clues complement semantic gradients. *The Reading Teacher, 61,* 249–254.

Hart, B., & Risley, T. (1995). *Meaningful differences in the everyday lives of young American children*. Baltimore: Paul H. Brookes.

Ivey, G., & Broaddus, K. (2001). Just plain reading: A survey of what makes students want to read in middle school classrooms. *Reading Research Quarterly, 36*, 350-377.

Juel, C., Biancarosa, G., Coker, D., & Deffes, R. (2003). Walking with Rosie: A cautionary tale of early reading instruction. *Educational Leadership, 60*, 12–18.

Manning, G. L., & Manning, M. (1984). What models of recreational reading make a difference? *Reading World, 23*, 375–389.

Marzano, R. J. (2004). *Building background knowledge for academic achievement*. Alexandria, VA: Association for Supervision and Curriculum Development.

Moore, D.W., Moore, S. A, Cunningham, P. M. & Cunningham, J. W. (2006). *Developing readers and writers in the content areas* (5th ed.). New York: Longman.

National Council for the Social Studies. (1994). *Expectations of excellence: Curriculum standards for social studies*. Washington, DC: Author.

National Council of Teachers of Mathematics. (2000). *Principles and standards for school mathematics*. Reston, VA: Author.

National Research Council. (1996). *National science education standards*. Washington, DC: National Academy Press.

Palmer, B. M., Codling, R. M., & Gambrell, L. B. (1994). In their own words: What elementary children have to say about motivation to read. *The Reading Teacher, 48*, 176–179.

Shefelbine, J. (1990). Student factors related to variability in learning word meanings from context. *Journal of Reading Behavior, 22*, 71–97.

Smith, Deb. (2001). My "high risk" students love reading real books. In P. M. Cunningham & D. P. Hall (Eds.), *True stories from four blocks classrooms* (pp. 23–32). Greensboro, NC: Carson-Dellosa.

Stahl, S. A., & Nagy, W. (2006). *Teaching word meanings*. Mahwah, NJ: Erlbaum.

Taba, H. (1967). *Teacher's handbook for elementary social studies*. Reading, MA: Addison-Wesley.

Yopp, R. H., & Yopp, K. Y. (2007). Ten important words plus: A strategy for building word knowledge. *The Reading Teacher, 61*, 157–160.

Index